Think Black, The Manifesto

MW01088632

Acknowledgements

Let me begin by acknowledging the Creator and Ancestors for instilling in me the intellectual curiosity to question and search for truth. For my parents in which I have two sets, Jasper Martin and Paula Mims for giving me life, Annette Dicks and Harvey Blount for nourishing my curiosity and allowing me to use my God-given talents that have become the lifeblood and foundation that I stand upon today as a person and as a man. I also express my deepest gratitude to Kai Nkosi and Russell Ligon for convincing me to continue to explore, develop, and write about a topic that I am deeply passionate. There are many other people along the way who've been encouraging me and have helped me to fulfill my purpose. I also thank Ronnie Burnett Sr., the producer of my Urban Politician radio show, who has never let me quit. Think Black, is a concept much bigger then myself, I don't own it, but I lay claim to it every single day. I pray that you may find inspiration and wisdom in this manifesto.
To all my family and friends, who have encouraged me along the way… You know who you are…
Asante Sana

Introduction

As far back as I can remember I never fully embraced the formal education that I received and neither did my spirit, since there was something unsettling about it although I never really understood why. Today, I am grateful for that uneasiness and what was once confusion and a lack of identity with what I had been taught has turned into a lifelong journey, my journey for truth. "Who am I" has became the underlying question in all that I began to seek.

Today, as an older, much more mature man who understands a bit more concerning our history, two key overwhelming thoughts comes to mind concerning the survival of our people. The first point is to understand that you can't separate our history from our spirituality. The second point is that once we understand that our history and spirituality are bound together, we know that the walls that divide us must crumble into tiny little pieces. We don't have to agree on every point; however we are forever connected by our mere existence on the earth. Therefore, we must forge together as one. Franz Fanon defines it this way,

"Each generation must out of relative obscurity discover its mission, fulfill it, or betray it."

Think Black…It's Okay, the manifesto is also the beginning of Think Black…It's Okay, the book, which will detail the benefits of changing our present destructive habits and adopting a culturally conscious concept and worldview that some might find revolutionary. Think Black…It's Okay, the book, will include insights and a discussion on what it means to Think Black…It's Okay in the vital disciplines such as economics, communications, media, law and justice, politics, finance, education, belief systems, the arts, history and health systems.

Think Black
It's Okay
~

The Manifesto

"To be political in an Afrikan-centered manner is to be concerned with the group interest, not individual gain or ambition"

~Mama Marimba Ani

Collective self-preservation is not a new concept. From our earliest beginnings people have organized into distinctive social groups for protection, survival, and perpetual self-preservation. While there are distinguishing differences between clans, tribes, ethnicity, and cultural practices, the single thread that binds them together is their common racial identity. This shared racial identity trumps all else when it comes to the survival and growth of a people. A collective racial identify is not random, but is God given, and should dictate how a people educate their children and build their economies. To "Think Black" is to adapt a worldview or perspective of viewing one's reality first and foremost with respect to race. The 7 Guiding Principles in the conceptualization of Think Black are represented by Truth, Justice, Righteousness, Order, Harmony, Balance, and Reciprocity.

First, the development of a Black Afrikan worldview is critical to the fostering of a great pride and awareness of the historical achievement and therefore the future of our distinct cultural intelligence in the minds of all members of our race, particularly our children. Secondly, the establishment of a Black Afrikan worldview is necessary to ordering the foundation and pillars of our healthy and thriving black communities. Thirdly, the development of a Black Afrikan worldview is necessary to establish and to maintain vital disciplines such as economics, communications, media, law and justice, politics, finance, education, belief systems, the arts, history and health systems, thereby creating a veil of protections and security around the advancement of our communities and society. Lastly, the promotion of a Black Afrikan worldview identifies the resting potential of our people to empower themselves through cooperative and collaborative partnerships and business enterprises, while building infrastructure and unlimited possibilities for urban strength and vitality.

We live in a multicultural society, one that espouses diversity on one hand, while racism on the other. Diversity is an interesting word since it implies inclusion and equality among the parts that make up the whole. All races are encouraged to participate in this façade of diverse equality, however, for Blacks, equality is never fully realized. While multiculturalism in American society is encouraged, for most groups the ideals of diversity do not demand total assimilation or the abandonment of racial traditions. Neither does this American diversity demand a rejection of a unique racial culture or worldview. Nevertheless, Blacks have voluntarily abandoned solidarity, dismissed traditional cultural awareness, and have chosen materialism and the unreality of racial equality over a collective effort toward the self-preservation of our community.

Various races have flourished in this nation by banning together, protecting their interests, and building strong community economies. For instance, Jewish, Chinese, Korean, and Latino's have not only brought their culture into this diverse society; but they have also built their own cultural economy inside the overall economy. Each of these racial groups teaches and maintains the unique history of their people to their own children. They maintain their cultural continuity through economics, history, education, and the arts. These acts of cultural self preservation are not seen as radical or defiant. The tactics of these racial groups are not seen as threatening, but are viewed as practical means of uplifting their race. This is common sense.

The concept of Think Black was adopted to address these issues within the Black community both in America and throughout the Diaspora. Why is it that we fail to see the world through our own racial and cultural lens? What do we do to further the cause of our collective survival and viability? These are the questions we must begin to address moving forward as a people. We have turned our backs on the Afrikan traditions of collectivism. We have opted for gross individualism and consumerism. We have deserted our inner cities and dismissed any responsibility to the overall wellness of our people. Our indifference is an indication of the depth of our disconnection from our people, our history, and ourselves.

THINK BLACK AFFIRMATIONS

- Since my stability, freedoms, and future are tied together with my Brothers and Sisters, I will view them as a reflection of myself. We will only be as strong as our weakest link.

- I will commit to learning and studying the history of our people and cultures. I will pass this knowledge on to my children and their children. I will not allow any outside group to invent the story of our people.

- I will adopt a collective value system of self-help, self- worth, and self-determination, and will teach our children accordingly, breaking the cycles of despair, self-hate, and shame.

- I will stop supporting entities that don't have our higher collective interest at heart including music, television shows, political factions and ideology, businesses, organizations, and individuals contributing to the negative images and perceptions of Black men, women, and children. I will reject entertainment and images that diminish Black genius, Black families, and Black love.

- I will stop making excuses for failing to spend money in our communities.

- I will be intentional in seeking out viable Black owned businesses in my community in an effort to support and encourage them to grow and expand.

- I will set aside a portion of my assets to support Black non-profit organizations heavily invested in building people and infrastructure in our community.

- I will support our Independently Black owned schools, since they are doing a yeomen's job educating our children. I will take the time to research what an Afrikan Centered education means and how it benefits our children. I will discover ways to offer my professional expertise, gifts, and talents to support Black owned schools in my community.

- I will encourage my church, mosque, or social organization to find ways to support the black community. I will encourage leadership and membership in such organizations to contribute financially and practically to addressing the needs of homelessness, drug abuse, HIV/AIDS, violence, domestic violence, unemployment, neglected seniors, teen pregnancy, fatherlessness, illiteracy, crippling poverty, hunger, mental illness and other deeply rooted and complex issues in my community that need our collective and immediate attention.

- I will daily check myself of my indifference and dismissal of the acute conditions plaguing our community, and hold myself accountable to take action and to encourage others to do the same.

Now it's time for us to emerge from the racial, cultural, economic, sociological and psychological captivity of the past 500 years and move towards the inauguration of a new and forward-thinking perspective on what it means to collectively and progressively Think Black.

It's Okay, It really is…

"Two men in a burning house must not stop to argue."

-Ashanti proverb

The Fabled City of Pali

Retold by Ishakamusa Barashango

There was a traveler who had gone around the world He had been to many different countries. One day he was in the western portion of *Alkebu-lan and he came across a city named Pali.

As he stumbled upon this city, he walked from one end of it to the other and spent all day there. His mouth opened in amazement because he has never seen anything like this in all of his travels throughout the world. He had seen many things, having traveled and studied different cultures, cities, and nations. He kept walking around shaking his head because he could not believe what he saw. Finally, he saw a venerable old man in the direction of the setting sun. As he was moving along, he said to the man, "Sir, please forgive me for disturbing you."

The elder said, "What can I do for you, my brother"?

He said, "Look, I'm perplexed. I need you to help me. I'm wondering if I got sunstroke as I was traveling or maybe I'm suffering from some type of hallucination. What kind of experience am I having?"

The elder, not quite understanding the traveler, said, "Just what is it? What is happening with you, my son?"

"Well, I have traveled this whole city and every place I went, I saw fine homes, every one of them looked like mansions. Everybody in the city is dressed well, they wear their finest **kinte cloth. They have a look on their face – a glow of happiness. They seem to be prosperous. They look healthy. The children are safe. I see them everywhere, all over the city. I have not been able to find one piece of trash on the streets. I have not found one poor person in the whole city. Not one beggar! Now that cannot be! Everywhere I have traveled in this world, you have the rich, a middle class, and on the bottom, you always have the impoverished. No matter where I go, this is the case. Even on this great continent of Alkebu-lan I have experienced this. This is the only city I have ever visited where I have not had that experience."

It was a shock to the traveler and he just couldn't seem to understand. "What I'm seeing," he continued, "is that everybody in this city is wealthy! Is
this true?!"

"Yes, they are," replied the elderly man.

The traveler replied, "But how can this be? How did you all accomplish this?" The elderly man replied, "Well sir, whenever someone comes to this great city of
Pali and they desire to become a resident, we meet in council. The

Council of Elders and the Mothers of the City come together. We interview the person and present them with questions. After our spiritual priest and priestesses observe the person, we meet again in a closed session. If we decide that this person has the kind of character we would want in our community and that they will bring something of value to this community, then we accept them as a resident. On the day that we welcome them into the city of Pali, there is a large gathering and celebration. Everybody brings a brick and a dollar."

The traveler asked, "Well… how many residents do you have?"

The elderly man thought for a moment. "Just over 100,000. So on the day you are welcomed into the city, each person presents you with a brick and a dollar.

When you come here, you start out with a mansion and $100,000.

**THINK
CULTURE**

FAMOUS SPEECHES FROM OUR GREAT LEADERS

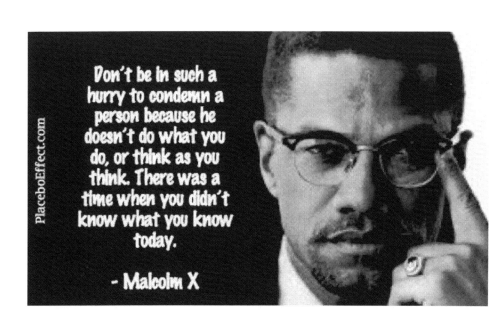

Don't be in such a hurry to condemn a person because he doesn't do what you do, or think as you think. There was a time when you didn't know what you know today.

- Malcolm X

PlaceboEffect.com

Police Brutality and the Mainstream Media
Speech in Los Angeles Malcolm X
May 5, 1962

In the Name of Allah, the Beneficent, the Merciful, to whom all praise is due, whom we forever thank for giving us the Honorable Elijah Mohammad as our leader, teacher, and guide. And I specifically, ladies and gentlemen, and brothers and sisters, open up like that because I am a representative of the Honorable Elijah Mohammad. And were it not for him, you and I wouldn't be her today.

In order for you and me to devise some kind of method or strategy to offset some of the events or the repetition of the events that have taken place in Los Angeles recently, we have to go to the root. We have to go to the cause. Dealing with the condition itself is not enough. We have to get to the cause of it all. Or the root of it all. And it is because of our effort toward getting straight to the root that people often times think we're dealing in hate. But first, I would like to congratulate and give to the Negro, so-called Negro leaders and so-called Negro organizations and excuse me if I say so-called, it's hard for me to just outright say Negro when I know what the word Negro really means.

The person whom you have come to know as Ronald Stokes, we know him as Brother Ron one for the most religious persons to display the highest form of morals of any Black person anywhere on this Earth. And as one of the previous speakers pointed out, who knew him, everyone who knew him had to give him credit for being a good man. A clean man, an intelligent man, and an innocent man when he was murdered.

The Negro, so-called Negro, organizations and leaders should be given great credit for their failure or refusal to let the white man divide them and use them, one against the other, during this crisis. As Reverend [Walkard] Wilson pointed out, I think it was eight years ago today, that the Supreme court handed down the desegregation decision. And despite the fact that eight years have gone past, that decision hasn't been implemented yet.

I don't have much faith.

I don't have that much confidence. I don't have that much patience.

And I don't have that much ignorance to…

If the Supreme Court, which is the highest lawmaking body in the country, can pass a decision that can't get even eight percent compliance within eight years, because it's for Black people, then my patience has run out.

When Black people who are being deprived of their citizenship... not only of their civil rights, but their human rights, become impatient, become fed up, don't wanna wait any longer, then they say it's emotional.

The Negro, so-called Negro, leaders and organizations should be praised. They should be congratulated. They should be complimented because out of all of them combined the white man has not yet found one who will play the role of Uncle Tom. But yet, he has found not Tom, no puppet, no parrot, who is still dumb enough in 1962 to represent the injustices that he is inflicting against our people.

We don't care what your religion is. We don't care what organization you belong to. We don't care how far in school you went or didn't go. We don't care the kind of job you have. We have to give you credit for shocking the white man by not letting him divide you and use you one against the other.

In the past, the greatest weapon the white man has had has been his ability to divide and conquer. As Jackie Robinson pointed out beautifully on the television last night, 4/5 of the world isn't white. Isn't' that what Jackie said? And if 4/5 of the world is dark, how is it possible for 1/5 to rule, oppress, exploit, dominate, and brutalize the 4/5 who are in the majority? How did they do it? Divide and conquer.

If I take my hand and slap you, you don't even feel it. It might sting you, because these digits get separated. But all I have to do to put you back in your place is bring those digits together. This is what the white man has done to you and me. He has divided us one against the other. But today, thanks to Allah, you can say thanks to God, or thanks to Jesus, or thanks to Jehovah, whatever you want.
But as a follower of the Honorable Elijah Mohammed, we have been taught to say thanks to Allah. He said, "Allah! [speaks Arabic]" I believe what's good for Jesus is good for you. If Allah was good enough for Jesus to call upon, I think he should be good enough for you to call upon.

Since the so called Negro community has shocked the white man by resisting all efforts to divide us, I think that you and I should continue to shock him by singing and working together in unity. Despite religious, political economic, or educational or social differences, let us remember that we are not brutalized because we are Baptist. We're not brutalized because we're Methodists. We're not brutalized because we are Muslim. We're not brutalized because we're

Catholic. We're brutalized because we are Black people in America. Here your mother is being raped, and you're not supposed to be emotional. Your women, your woman can't walk the street without some cracker putting his hands on her, and you're not supposed to be emotional.

If you say that you're fed up, if you teach the Negro they don't even know their name---What? Because he took it away from us. 20 million Black people who don't even know their history of their ancestors. Why? Because he took it away from us! And if you try and tell them how thoroughly and completely they've been robbed, he says, you're teaching hate. That's something to think about. Today we're coming out of college; you're coming out of the leading universities. You're trying to go in a good direction. But you don't know which direction to go in. And if somebody tries to take you right to the root of your problem, they say that that man's a hate teacher. If I ask why should the Senators in Washington— And then again, if we tell you that the Negro are being hung on a tree, or being shot down illegally, unjustly... and those Negros should do something to protect themselves you say you're advocating violence. The white man is tricking you! He's trapping you. He doesn't call it violence when he lands troops in Berlin. When the Japanese attack Pearl Harbor, he didn't get non-violent. He said, "Praise the Lord, but pass the ammunition."

But when someone attacks you, when someone comes at you with a gun, despite the fact that you've done nothing, he tells you, "Suffer peacefully." "Pray for those who use you to spite me." "Be long suffering." And how long can you suffer after suffering for 400 years. So I just wanna play up that little point right there because he said that we play on your emotions. And when you turn on your television tonight, or your radio, or read the newspaper, they're gonna tell you in that paper that I was playing on your emotions. Imagine you, a second class citizen. That's not getting emotional! It's getting intelligent.

And as far as your mayor is concerned, I see- should say their mayor. A man named Yorty, whose been slandering the Muslims, a professional liar—a professional liar. Who has mastered the art of using half-truths. Put in the paper that they break into our religious place of worship and got records that they can use to prove that most of us have a criminal record. Martin Luther King has been to jail. James Farmer has been to jail.

Why, you can't name a black man in this country who was sick and tired of the hell that he's catching who hasn't been to jail. Why, you haven't got a man of God in the Bible that wasn't put to jail when they started speaking up against exploitation and oppression. They charged Jesus with sedition.

Didn't they do that? They said he was against Caesar. They said he was discriminating because he told his disciples, "Go not the way of the gentiles, but rather go to the lost sheep." He discriminated. Don't go near the gentiles, go to the lost sheep. Go to the oppressed. Go to the down trodden. Go to the exploited. Go to the people who don't know who they are, who are lost from the knowledge of themselves and who are strangers in a land that is not theirs. Go to those people! Go to the slaves. Got to the second class citizens. Go to the ones who are suffering the brunt of Caesar's brutality.

And if Jesus were here in America today, he wouldn't be going to the white man. The white man is the oppressor! He would be going to the humble. He would be going to the lowly. He would be going to the rejected and the despised. He would be going to the so called American Negro.

To have once been a criminal is no disgrace. To remain a criminal is the disgrace. I formally was a criminal. I formally was in prison. I'm not ashamed of that. You never can use that over my head. And he's using the wrong stick! I don't feel that stick. I went to prison because I believed in men like Sam Yorty. But since I've been following the Honorable Elijah Mohammad, I have been reformed and that's more than Sam Yorty and Chief Parker and all these other white politicians that have been able to do with the inmates in the prisons of this state.

They should give Mr. Muhammad credit. They should give Mr. Muhammad credit for reforming and rehabilitating men whom they have failed to reform and rehabilitate. Mayor Yorty went forward to some press report that Mr. Muhammad had once been found guilty of contributing to delinquency of a minor. He failed to explain, purposely, that in 1934, the Honorable Elijah Muhammad refused to send his children to white school in Detroit, Michigan, that were teaching you about the little black Sambo. That's the minor that he contributed to the delinquency of.

You see this vicious, fork-tongued white man has been able to take lies and make you turn against those who want to help you and make others turn against you. This is the contributing to the delinquency of a minor that this mayor, or a man who calls himself mayor, is talking about. In the same article he said that the Muslims are the same people who rioted in the United Nations. Someone should pull his coat and let him know that at the present moment there's six million dollars' worth of suits level against two of the New York's leading newspapers for making a mistake of charging the Muslims as being involved in the those United Nations riots. We were not involved! And this fork-tongued man who calls himself your mayor had taken the time to find that out, he wouldn't be walking into the trap that he's letting his ignorance lead him into! And if you take the time to read the Washington Post, that came out the Sunday after that incident took place, the Washington Post pointed out on the front page that the Muslims had nothing to do with the UN riots and they quoted in saying is, the person who was at that time the Commissioner of Police in New York City.

See, it's lies the white man has spread about Muslims to try and make you afraid of the Muslims, or to try and make you think that the Muslims were a criminal element, an uncouth element a thing that you have not liked to be associated with. Also, they say that, I'm just clearing these things up and we're going to get into what happened. They also say that the Honorable Elijah Muhammad was a draft dodger. No, he wasn't. He just refused to go to the army because he was a man of peace. He was a minister of religion of peace. He was teaching peace. So he outright refused to go to the army. That's not draft dodging. That's intelligence.

Here, before the grand jury, because the coroner's jury is stacked against Negros. The grand jury is stacked against Negros. The press, the radio, the television and the newspapers are stacked against Negros. But, Los Angeles Police Department is stacked against Negros, all except those he has appointed to high positions. The control press, the white press inflames the white public against Negros. The police are able to use it to paint the Negro community as a criminal element. The police are able to use the press to make the white public think that 90%, or 99% of the Negroes in the Negro community are criminals.

And once white public is convinced that most of the Negro community is a criminal element, then this automatically paves the way for the police to move into the Negro community exercising Gestapo tactics stopping any Black man who is in this— on the sidewalk, whether he is guilty or whether he is innocent. Whether he is well dressed or whether he is poorly dressed. Whether he is educated or whether he is dumb. Whether he's Christian or whether he's a Muslim. As long as he is Black and a member of the Negro community, the white public thinks that the white policeman is justified in going in there and trampling on that man's civil rights and that man's human rights.

Once the police have convinced the white public that the so called Negro community is a criminal element, they can go in and question, brutalize, murder, unarmed innocent Negros and the white public is gullible enough to back them up. This makes the Negro community a police state. This makes the Negro neighborhood a police state. It's the most heavily patrolled. It has more police in it than any other neighborhood, yet is has more crime in it than any other neighborhood. How can you have more cops and more crime? It shows that cops must be in cahoots with the criminals.

The texture of the hair that God-that god gave them so much that they put lye on it. Do you realize brother now, you know brother; lye will eat a hole in steel and you know your head is not that hard. Who taught you. Who taught you to hate the texture of your hair? Who taught you to hate the color of your skin to such an extent that you bleach to get it like the white man? Who taught you to hate the shape of your nose and the shape of your lips? Who taught you to hate yourself from the top of your head to the soles of your feet? Who taught you to hate your own kind? Who taught you to hate the race that you belong to? So much so that you don't want to be around each other.

You know, before you come asking Mr. Muhammed does he teach hate, you should ask yourself, who taught you to hate being what God gave you. We teach you to love the hair that God gave you. Here you way out in the middle of the ocean, can't swim, and you worried about someone that's in the bathtub and can't swim.

We don't steal. Wed don't gamble. We don't lie, and we don't cheat. And that also deprives the government of revenue because you can't get into a whiskey bottle without getting past the government seal. You can't open a deck of cards without getting past the government seal.. Hell, the white man makes the whiskey then puts you in jail for getting drunk. He sells you the cards and the dice and puts you in jail when he catches you using 'em. So, he's against us because we fix it where he can't catch you anymore. We take the dice outta your hands the cards out of your hands and the whiskey out of your head.

The most disrespected person in America is the black woman. The most unprotected person in America is the black woman. The most neglected person in America is the black woman. And as Muslims,

the Honorable Elijah Muhammad teaches us to respect our women. And the only time a Muslim really gets real violent is when someone goes to molest his woman. We will kill you for our woman. We believe that if the white man will do whatever is necessary to see that his woman gets respect and protection then you and I will never be recognized as men until we stand up like men and place the same penalty over the head of anyone who puts his filthy hands in the direction of our women. We respect them, but we want them to respect us. We think the law should respect the Negro community.
The law should approach the Negro community with intelligence if it expects the Negro community to react intelligently. So the Honorable Elijah Muhammed teaches us to always avoid anything that smacks of disrespect for the law. And if the police department tells the truth, it will have to admit that they never had any, uh, experiences with Muslims have ever been anything other than honorable unless they themselves come at us in a dishonorable way.

There's no case against the Muslims. It has no case against these brothers whom they shot down. And because it has no case, it's trying to create a case. It's trying to manufacture a case. And therefore they set up a grand jury hearing of the case so that they could hear it behind closed doors, and after hearing what we have to say then they'll- their particular strategy of defense against the actions that they committed on that April the 27th. So, at the advice of our attorneys, we purposefully, the victims, those who have been indicted, or rather those who have been arrested and are out on bond have purposefully refrained and refused from making any statement whatsoever until after the case appears in court.
And when you hear their story it will be in a public trial. We have already been, had experience with these private hearings behind closed doors. Anything that the white man has to do to the Muslim, he has to do it in the open. He has to do it in public, or he has to put every single one of us behind bars for the rest of our lives.
When Mayor Yorty called for a government investigation of a religious group that have the highest moral standards of any group on the Negro community, Mayor Yorty was giving you an example of what Hitler did in Nazi Germany when he began to go on the rampage.
We feel, we have confidence that the white public and the Black public, if they hear our case, if they heard and have access to the investigation, will never be fooled by this phoney set up that's

stacked from the top all the way down. And if you doubt it, when you leave here tonight, when you go home tonight, look for the press. I'd like at this time to call forth these brothers who are under, uh, who were arrested. The brothers who were arrested. Come up here behind these chairs please. They were suspect.

This wouldn't happen in a white neighborhood. White men can walk down the street with packages on his head packages under his arm and packages anywhere else and won't anybody question his right to carry those packages. But a Negro is suspect because the press makes you suspect. Yes, the white press makes the Negro suspect. All the information you need, Officer. And the Officer made one stay at the rear fo the cared and the other go to the front of the care and while he was taking the one to the front of the care, the polite attitude, the humble, the submissive, intelligent peaceful spirit that he unexpectedly found in this Negro infuriated him.

And he began to hold the brother, 'put down your hands'. Brother was talking, he's not a criminal. A man has a right on the sidewalk to talk with his hands. 'Put down your hands, don't talk with your hands.' And when the brother continued to gesture with his hands the officer grabbed his hand, twisted it around behind his back, flung him up against the car and then that's when hell broke loose. A struggle ensued, shots were fired by the police and by a Negro door shaker.

An alarm went out. When the alarm went out, instead of the police going to the place where the incident occurred, the police went a block away to the temple. When they arrived there, they got out of their cars with their guns smoking. You woulda thought it was Wyatt, what's his name? Wyatt Earp. I'm telling you, they came out of those cars and we have enough witnesses to hang 'em. With their guns smoking. Chief Parker knows this, Mayor Yorty knows this and every police official in the city knows that.

They didn't fire no warning shots in the air they fired warning shots point blank at innocent, unarmed, defenseless Negros. As I say, two of the brothers were shot in the back. Another was shot, two of them were shot, excuse the expression through the penis. Another was shot in the hip and the bullet came out the other side. But Arthur was shot ¼ of an inch from his heart.

Let me tell you something, and I'll tell you why you say, 'we hate white people.' We don't hate anybody. We love our own so much, they think we hate the ones who are inflicting injustice against them. Who has been shot, the bullet having passed a ¼ of an inch through his heart. I'm not gonna let him talk, which I think you can understand why. You should listen to the conversation of the police officers while it was going on.

Two of the brothers who had been shot who were lying hand in hand, the officer said they were chanting a death chant. You read that. They were saying, 'Allah U Akbar.' What does that mean? It means that God is the greatest. God is the greatest.   And it shook the officer up that they haven't heard Black people talk any kinda talk but what they taught 'em. And two of the brothers were shot in the back were telling me that as they lay on the sidewalk, they were holding hands. They held hands with each other saying, Allah U Akbar. And the blood was seeping go f of them where the police bullets had torn into their insides. Still, they said Allah U Akbar and the police came and kicked them in the head. Policed kicked them in the head telling them to shut up that noise while they were lying on the sidewalk in front of the temple. Kicked them in the head. Shut up that noise.

And one of them, when he was on his way to the police station in the ambulance, one of the ambulance attendants told the white cop, 'why don't you kill the nigger?' He said, 'I'll tell them that he tried to get away. Why don't you kill the nigger?

While you got a chance. I'll swear that he tried to get away.' If he didn't say this, then I need to go be put in jail, and I'll gladly go. One of them who was being taken to jail in a police car as the ambulance sirens were coming to the place, one of the policeman said to the other: 'What are the ambulances rushing for? Nothing but some niggers.' So, he looked then and saw the Muslim brothers sitting beside him and he shut up. But after he got to the jail, the same officer that said this turned to the brother and said, 'I hope that you didn't get offended by what I said back there under the heat of emotion, because some of my best friends are colored.' That's what he said. That's his password: 'Some of my best friends are colored.'

And I for one, as a Muslim, believe that the white man is intelligent enough, if he were made to realize how Black people really feel and how fed up we are without that whole compromising sweet talk. Why you're the one that make it hard for yourself. The white man believes you when you go to him with that old sweet talk 'cause you been sweet talkin' him ever since he brought you here. Stop sweet talking him. Tell him how you feel. Tell him how or what kinda hell you been catching and let him know that if he's not ready to clean his house up if he shouldn't have a house. It should catch on fire. And burn down.

As Muslims, we identify ourselves with the dark world. So, we're not any minority. We're a part of the majority and the white man is the minority. You to know this to understand us. We don't think any odds are against us. We don't fight a battle

like the odds are against us. Why, the whole dark world today is in unity. It's one. If you don't think so, look at the United Nations. When the dark world votes, they vote as one. They getting colonialists out of African and out of Asia. Tellin' them to get out. They don't have any nuclear weapons but they got solid, united voice and their unity alone is sufficient to drive the oppressor and exploiter of their people out of their own country. You and I need to learn a lesson from that right there.

In the UN, the dark world consists of Buddhists, Hindus, Shinto, Taoists, Christians, Muslims, everything. But they're together. They forget their religious and political differences. They think as one. They move as one against a common enemy. And [inaudible' of Algeria, he's going, don't think he's not going, he's going. They're getting gout of Angola, out of Uganda, out of Kenya. He's going from South Africa too. He hasn't got long to be there. All over this earth, dark people who have been oppressed and exploited by those how are not their own kind, strangers, are coming together to get the oppressor off their back. You and I learn a lesson from that.

We are oppressed. We are exploited. We are downtrodden. We are denied, not only civil rights, but even human rights. So the only way we're going to get some of this oppression and exploitation away from us or aside from us is to come together against the common enemy. When they sat down at the Bandung conference, everyone there had this in common: a dark skin. Some of those who were sitting there were socialists, some were communists, some were capitalists, some were Christian, some were Buddhist. They were everything! But all of 'em was dark skinned. And they looked at the dark skin and agreed that this one thing they had in common. Forget you're a Methodist, forget that you're a catholic, forget that you're Protestant , forget that you're a Muslim. Remember that all of us are Black and we're catching hell.

THINK
CHANGE

James Baldwin
MY DUNGEON SHOOK
Letter To My Nephew
On The One Hundredth Anniversary Of The Emanicipation
December 1962

Dear James:

I have begun this letter five times and torn it up five times. I keep seeing your face, which is also the face of your father and my brother. Like him, you are tough, dark, vulnerable, mood—with a very definite tendency to sound truculent because you want no one to think you are soft. You may be like your grandfather in this, I don't know, but certainly both you and your father resemble him very much physically. Well, he is dead, he never saw you, and he had a terrible life; he was defeated long before he died because, at the bottom of his heart, he really believed what white people said about him. This is one of the reasons that he became so holy. I am sure that your father has told you something about all that. Neither you nor your father exhibit any tendency towards holiness: you really are of another era, part of what happened when the late E. Franklin Frazier called "the

cities of destruction." You can only be destroyed by believing that you really are what the white world calls a nigger. I tell you this because I love you, and please don't forget it.

I have known both of you all your lives, have carried your Daddy in my arms and on my shoulders, kissed and spanked him and watched him learn to walk. I don't know if you've known anybody from that far back; if you've loved anybody that long, first as an infant, then as a child, then as a man, you gain a strange perspective on time and human pain and effort. Other people cannot see what I see whenever I look into your father's face as it is today are all those other faces which were his. Let him laugh and I see a cellar your father does not remember and a house he does not remember and I hear in his present laughter his laughter as a child. Let him curse and I remember him falling down the cellar steps, and howling, and I remember, with pain, his tears, which my hand or your grandmother's so easily wiped away. But no one's hand can wipe away those tears he sheds invisibly today, which one hears in his laughter and in his speech and in his songs. I know what the world has done to my brother and how narrowly he has survived it.

And I know, which is much worse, and this is the crime of which I accuse my country and my countrymen, and for which neither I nor time nor history will ever forgive them, that they have destroyed and are destroying hundreds of thousands of lives and do not know it and do not want to know it. One can be, indeed one must strive to become, tough and philosophical concerning destruction and death, for this is what most of mankind has been best at since we have heard of man. (But remember: most of mankind is not all of mankind.) But it is not permissible that the authors of devastation should also be innocent. It is the innocence which constitutes the crime.

Now, my dear namesake, these innocent and well-meaning people, your countrymen, have caused you to be born under conditions not very far removed from those described for us by Charles Dickens in the London of more than a hundred years ago. (I hear the chorus of the innocents screaming, "No! This is not true! How bitter you are!"—but I am writing this letter to you, to try to tell you something about how to handle them, for most of them do not yet really know that you exist. I know the conditions, under which you were born, for I was there. Your countrymen were not there, and haven't made it yet. Your grandmother was also there, and no one has ever accused her of being bitter. I suggest that the innocents check with her. She isn't hard to find. Your countrymen don't know that she exists, either, though she has been working for them all their lives.)

Well, you were born, here you came, something like fourteen years ago: and though your father and mother and grandmother, looking about the streets

through which they were carrying you, staring at the walls into which they brought you, had every reason to be heavyhearted, yet they were not. For here you were, Big James, named for me—you were a big baby, I was not—here you were: to be loved. To be loved, baby, hard, at once, and forever, to strengthen you against the loveless world. Remember that: I know how black it looks today, for you. It looked bad that day, too, yes, we were trembling. We have not stopped trembling yet, but if we had not loved each other none of us would have survived. And now you must survive because we love you, and for the sake of your children and your children's children.

This innocent country set you down in a ghetto in which, in fact, it intended that you should perish. Let me spell out precisely what I mean by that, for the heart of the matter is here, and the root of my dispute with my country. You were born where you were born, and faced the future that you faced because you were black and for no other reason. The limits of your ambition were, thus, expected to be set forever. You were born into a society which spelled out with brutal clarity, and in as many ways as possible, that you were a worthless human being. You were not expected to aspire to excellence: you were expected to make peace with mediocrity. Wherever you have turned, James, in your short time on this earth , you have been told where you could go and what you could do (and how you could do it) and where you could do it and whom you could marry. I know that your countrymen do not agree with me about this, and I hear them saying "You exaggerate." They do not know Harlem, and I do. So do you. Take no one's word for anything, including mine—but trust your experience. Know whence you came.

If you know whence your came, there is really no limit to where you can go. The details and symbols of your life have been deliberately constructed to make you believe what white people say about you. Please try to remember that what that believe, as well as what they do and cause you to endure, does not testify to your inferiority but to their inhumanity and fear. Please try to be clear, dear James, though the storm which rages about your youthful head today, about the reality which lies behind the words acceptance and integration. There is no reason for you to try to become like white people and there is no basis whatever for their impertinent assumption that they must accept you. The really terrible thing, old buddy, is that you must accept them. And I mean that very seriously. You must accept them and accept them with love. For these innocent people have no other hope. They are, in effect, still trapped in a history which they do not understand; and until they understand it, they cannot be released from it. They have had to believe for so many years, and for innumerable reasons, that black men are inferior to white men. Many of them, indeed, know better, but, as you will discover, people

find it very difficult to act on what they know. To act is to be committed, and to be committed is to be in danger. In this case, the danger, in the minds of most white Americans, is the loss of identity. Try to imagine how you would feel if you woke up one morning to find the sun shinning and all the stars aflame. You would be frightened because it is our of the order of nature. Any upheaval in the universe is terrifying because it so profoundly attacks one's sense of one's own reality. Well, the black man has functioned in the white man's world as a fixed star, as an immovable pillar: and as he moves out of his place, heaven and earth are shaken to their foundations. You, don't be afraid. I said that it was intended that you should perish in the ghetto, perish by never being allowed to go behind the white man's definitions, by never being allowed to spell your proper name. You have, and many of us have, defeated this intention; and, by a terrible law, a terrible paradox, those innocents who believed that your imprisonment made them safe are losing their grasp of reality.   But these

men are your brothers—your lost, younger brothers.
And if the word integration means anything, this is what it means: that we, with love, shall force our brothers to see themselves as they are, to cease fleeing from reality and begin to change it. For this is your home, my friend, do not be driven from it; great men have done great things here, and will again, and we can make America what America must become. It will be hard, James, but you come from sturdy, peasant stock, men who picked cotton and dammed rivers and built railroads, and in the teeth of the most terrifying odds, achieved and unassailable and monumental dignity. You come from a long line of poets, some of the greatest poets since Homer. One of them said, The very time I thought I was lost, My dungeon shook and my chains fell off.

You know, and I know, that the country is celebrating one hundred years of freedom one hundred years too soon. We cannot be free until they are free. God bless you, James, and Godspeed.

Your uncle, James

THINK
POWER

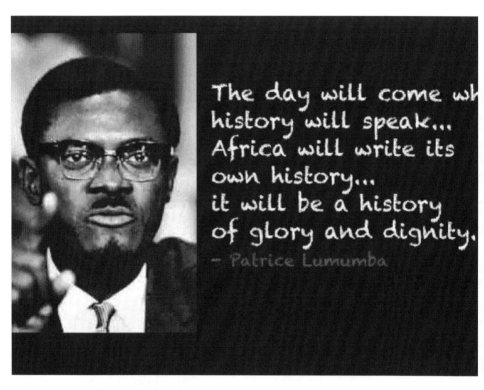

The day will come wh
history will speak...
Africa will write its
own history...
it will be a history
of glory and dignity.
– Patrice Lumumba

Patrice Lumumba
Speech at the Proclamation of Congolese Independence

June 30, 1960

Congolese men and women:
As combatants for independence who today are victorious, I salute
you in the name of the Congolese government. I ask all my friends,
all of you who have fought unceasingly at our side, to make this thir-
tieth of June, 1960, an illustrious date that will be indelibly engraved
upon your hearts, a date whose meaning you will teach your children
with pride, so that they in turn will tell their children and their children's children the glorious story of our struggle for freedom.
For though this independence of the Congo is today being proclaimed in a spirit of accord with Belgium, a friendly country with
which we are dealing as one equal with another, no Congolese wor-
thy of the name can ever forget that we fought to win it a fight waged
each and every day, a passionate and idealistic fight, a fight in which
there was not one effort, not one privation, not one suffering, not one
drop of blood that we ever spared ourselves.

We are proud of this struggle amid tears, fire, and blood, down
to our very heart of hearts, for it was a noble and just struggle, an
indispensable struggle if we were to put an end to the humiliating
slavery that had been forced upon us.

The wounds that are the evidence of the fate we endured for
eighty years under a colonialist regime are still too fresh and pain-
ful for us to be able to erase them from our memory. Back-breaking
work has been exacted from us, in return for wages that did not allow
us to satisfy our hunger, or to decently clothe or house ourselves, or
to raise our children as creatures very dear to us.

We have been the victims of ironic taunts, of insults, of blows
that we were forced to endure morning, noon, and night because we
were blacks. Who can forget that a black was addressed in the famil-
iar form, not because he was a friend, certainly, but because the polite
form of address was to be used only for whites? We have had our
lands despoiled under the terms of what was supposedly the law of
the land but was only recognition of the right of the strongest.
We have known that the law was quite different for whites and blacks;
it was most accommodating for the former, and cruel and inhuman
for the latter. We have known the atrocious sufferings of those ban-

ished to remote regions because of their political opinions or religious beliefs; exiles in their own country, their fate was truly worse than death. We have known that there were magnificent mansions for whites in the cities and ramshackle straw hovels for blacks, that a black was never allowed into the so-called European movie theaters or restaurants or stores; that a black traveled in the hold of boats below the feet of the white in his deluxe cabin. Who can forget, finally, the burst of rifle fire in which so many of our brothers perished, the cells into which the authorities threw those who no longer were willing to submit to a rule where justice meant oppression and exploitation?

We have grievously suffered all this, my brothers. But we who have been chosen to govern our beloved country by the vote of your elected representatives, we whose bodies and souls have suffered from colonialist oppression, loudly proclaim: all this is over and done with now. The Republic of the Congo has been proclaimed and our country is now in the hands of its own children. We are going to begin another struggle together, my brothers, my sisters, a sublime struggle that will bring our country peace, prosperity, and grandeur.

We are going to institute social justice together and ensure everyone just remuneration for his labor. We are going to show the world what the black man can do when, he works in freedom, and we are going to make the Congo the focal point for the development of all of Africa.

We are going to see to it that the soil of our country really benefits its children. We are going to review all the old laws and make new ones that will be just and noble.

We are going to put an end to the suppression of free thought and see to it that all citizens enjoy to the fullest all the fundamental freedoms laid down in the Declaration of the Rights of Man.

We are going to do away with any and every sort of discrimination and give each one the rightful place that his human dignity, his labor, and his devotion to the country will have earned him.

We are going to bring peace to the country, not the peace of rifles and bayonets, but the peace that comes from men's hearts and their good will.

And in order to achieve all this, dear compatriots, rest assured that we will be able to count not only on our tremendous strength and our immense riches, but also on the assistance of many foreign countries, whose collaboration we will always accept if it is sincere and does not seek to force any policy of any sort whatsoever on us.

In this regard, Belgium has finally realized what direction history was moving in and has not attempted to oppose our independence. She is ready to grant us her aid and her friendship, and a treaty to this effect has just been signed between our two equal and independent countries. I am certain that this cooperation will be beneficial to both countries. We for our part, though we shall continue to be vigilant, will respect all commitments freely made.

Thus the new Congo, our beloved republic that my government is going to create, will be a rich, free, and prosperous country, with regard to both its domestic relations and its foreign relations. But in order for us to reach this goal without delay, I ask all of you, Congolese legislators and citizens alike, to aid me with all the strength at your command.

I ask all of you to forget the trivial quarrels that are draining our strength and threaten to earn us the contempt of those in other countries.

I ask the parliamentary minority to aid my government by constructive opposition and to stay strictly within legal and democratic paths.

I ask all of you not to shrink from making any sacrifice necessary to ensure the success of our great undertaking.

I ask you, finally, to respect unconditionally the life and property of your fellow citizens and foreigners who have settled in our country. If the behavior of these foreigners leaves something to be desired, our justice will be swift and they will be expelled from the territory of the republic; if, on the other hand, they conduct themselves properly, they must be left in peace, for they too will be working for the prosperity of our country.

The independence of the Congo represents a decisive step toward the liberation of the entire African continent.

Your Majesty, Your Excellencies, Ladies and Gentlemen, my dear compatriots, my black brothers, my brothers in the struggle, that is what I wanted to say to you in the name of the government on this magnificent day of our complete and sovereign independence.

Our strong, national, popular government will be the salvation of this country. I invite all Congolese citizens, men, women, and children, to set to work to create a prosperous national economy that will be the crowning proof of our economic independence.
Honor to those who fought for national freedom! Long live independence and African unity!

Long live the independent and sovereign Congo!

ALL POWER
TO THE PEOPLE!

AIN'T I A WOMAN?

By Sojourner TruthDelivered 1851 at the Women's Convention in Akron, Ohio

Well, children, where there is so much racket there must be something out of kilter. I think that 'twixt the negroes of the South and the women at the North, all talking about rights, the white men will be in a fix pretty soon. But what's all this here talking about?

That man over there says that women need to be helped into carriages, and lifted over ditches, and to have the best place everywhere. Nobody ever helps me into carriages, or over mud-puddles, or gives me any best place! And ain't I a woman?

Look at me! Look at my arm! I have ploughed and planted, and gathered into barns, and no man could head me! And ain't I a woman? I could work as much and eat as much as a man - when I could get it - and bear the lash as well! And ain't I a woman? I have borne thirteen children, and seen most all sold off to slavery, and when I cried out with my mother's grief, none but Jesus heard me! And ain't I a woman?

Then they talk about this thing in the head; what's this they call it? [member of audience

whispers, "intellect"] That's it, honey. What's that got to do with women's rights or negroes' rights? If my cup won't hold but a pint, and yours holds a quart, wouldn't you be mean not to let me have my little half measure full?

Then that little man in black there, he says women can't have as much rights as men, 'cause Christ wasn't a woman! Where did your Christ come from? Where did your Christ come from? From God and a woman! Man had nothing to do with Him.

If the first woman God ever made was strong enough to turn the world upside down all alone, these women together ought to be able to turn it back , and get it right side up again! And now they is asking to do it, the men better let them
Obliged to you for hearing me, and now old Sojourner ain't got nothing more to say.

Angela Davis

Victory Speech delivered at the Embassy Auditorium
Los Angeles, California - June 9, 1972

It's really a wonderful feeling to be back among the people. [applause, cheers] To be back among all of you who fought so long and so hard, among all of you who actually achieved my freedom. And I really wish you could have been there in the courtroom at the moment when those three "not guilty" verdicts were pronounced, because that victory was just as much yours as it was mine. ["Right on!" applause] And as we laughed and cried, these were expressions of our joy as we witnessed what was a real people's victory and in spirit you were all there at that moment.

Over the last few days I've been literally overwhelmed with congratulations and expressions of solidarity, whether it's been in meetings or on the streets or in restaurants; in the black and brown communities in northern California, wherever I've gone I've been greeted with hugs and kisses and it's really been beautiful.

Even in a city like San Jose, among the white population, many people have come out and have congratulated me and have told me that actually, they were behind us all the time. And during these last days I have sensed a real feeling of unity and togetherness and a kind of collective enthusiasm which I have rarely experienced on such a massive scale.

And in the midst of all of this it's sort of difficult for me to grasp that I am the person around whom all of this enthusiasm has emerged. Yet because of it I feel that I have a special responsibility – a special responsibility to you who have stood with me in struggle. But sometimes I have to admit when I'm off by myself and I reflect on everything that has happened over the last two years, I really wonder whether or not I will be able to meet the role which history has cut out for me, which you have cut out for me, but I promise I am going to try. That, I promise.

When it all started – and I'm speaking of myself – when I experienced the first stirrings of a commitment to the cause of freedom, the last thing I envisioned at that time were ambitions to become a figure known to great numbers of people. At that time I was simply aspiring to do everything I could to give my meager talents and energies to the cause of my people; to the cause of black people and brown people; and to all racially oppressed, and economically oppressed people in this country and throughout the globe. But history doesn't always conform to our own personal desires. It doesn't always conform to the blueprints we set up for our lives.

My life, and the lives of my family, my mother, my comrades, my friends, has really been drastically transformed over the last two years. For what happened was that as our movement – and particularly our movement right here in Los Angeles, our movement to free political prisoners, our movement to free all oppressed people – as that movement began to grow and become stronger and develop in breadth, it just so happened that I was the one who – one of the ones who was singled out by the government's finger of repression. It just so happened that I was destined to become yet another symbol of what the government intends to do – what the government in this state would do to every person who refuses to be its passive, submissive subjects.

But then, but then came the surge of a massive popular resistance, then came thousands and thousands and hundreds of thousands of people who were rising up to save me as we had tried to rise up and save the Soledad Brothers and other political prisoners. And what happened was that the government's plan, the government's project of repression fell apart; it backfired. The government could not, through me, terrorize people who would openly demonstrate their opposition to racism, to war, to poverty, to repression.

And on the contrary, people let it be known that they would not be manipulated by terror. They would stand behind all their sisters and brothers who had been caught in the government's web of repression. I was one of those who were entrapped in that web. And the thousands and millions of people throughout the world came together in struggle and saved me from the fate the government had planned as an example to all of you who were disposed to resist. You intervened and saved my life, and now I am back among you, and as I was wrested away from you in struggle, so likewise I return in struggle. I return in struggle with a very simple message, a very simple message: We've just begun our fight. We've just begun.

And while we celebrate the victory of my own acquittal, and also of the release on appeal of a very beautiful brother from a Texas prison. I don't know if you know him, his name is Leotis Johnson.

He was a SNCC, SCLC organizer in Texas and was framed up on a marijuana charge. He was released just a few days ago after having spent four years, four years in a Texas prison. We have to celebrate that victory, too, but as we celebrate these victories, we must also be about the business of transforming our joy, our enthusiasm into an even deeper commitment to all our sisters and brothers who do not yet have cause to celebrate.

And as I say this, I remember very, very vividly the hundreds of women who were with me in the New York Women's House of Detention, most of them black and brown women, all of them from the poorest strata of this society. I remember the women in the sterile cells of Marin County Jail, and the women in the dimly lit, windowless cells in Santa Clara County. There is still the savage inhumanity of Soledad Prison. One Soledad brother, our brother George, has been murdered. The two who survived were recently acquitted, but hundreds more are awaiting our aid and solidarity.

There are hundreds and thousands of Soledad Brothers, or San Quentin Brothers, or Folsom Brothers, of CIW sisters, all of whom are prisoners of an insanely criminal social order. So let us celebrate, but let us celebrate in the only way that is compatible with all the pain and suffering that so many of our sisters and brothers must face each morning as they awake to the oppressive sight of impenetrable concrete and steel. As they awake to the harsh banging of heavy iron doors opening and closing at the push of a button. As they awake each morning to the inevitable jangling of the keepers' keys – keys which are a constant reminder that freedom is so near, yet so far away. Millenniums and millenniums away.

So let us celebrate in the only way that is fitting. Let the joy of victory be the foundation of an undying vow; a renewed commitment to the cause of freedom. For we know now that victories are possible, though the struggles they demand are long and arduous. So let our elation merge with a pledge to carry on this fight until a time when all the antiquated ugliness and brutality of jails and prisons linger on only as a mere, a mere memory of a nightmare. For our vow will be fulfilled only when we, or our children, or our grandchildren will have succeeded in seizing the reins of history, in determining the destiny of mankind and creating a society where prisons are unheard of because the racism and the exploitative economic arrangement which reproduces want for the many and wealth for the few will have become relics of a past era.

It has been said many times that one can learn a great deal about a society by looking towards its prisons. Look towards its dungeons and there you will see in concentrated and microcosmic form the sickness of the entire system. And today in the United States of America in 1972 there is something that is particularly revealing about the analogy between the prison and the larger society of which it is a reflection. For in a painfully real sense we are all prisoners of a society whose bombastic proclamations of freedom and justice for all are nothing but meaningless rhetoric.

For this society's accumulated wealth, its scientific achievements are swallowed up by the avarice of a few capitalists and by insane projects of war and other irrational ventures. We are imprisoned in a society where there is so much wealth and so many sophisticated scientific and technological skills that anyone with just a little bit of common sense can see the insanity of a continued existence of ghettos and barrios and the poverty which is there.

For when we see the rockets taking off towards the moon, and the B-52's raining destruction and death on the people of Vietnam, we know that something is wrong. We know that all we have to do is to redirect that wealth and that energy and channel it into food for the hungry, and to clothes for the needy; into schools, hospitals, housing, and all the material things that are necessary, all the material things that are necessary in order for human beings to lead decent, comfortablelives – in order to lead lives which are devoid of all the pressures of racism, and yes, male supremacist attitudes and institutions and all the other means with which the rulers manipulate the people. For only then can freedom take on a truly human meaning? Only then can we be free to live and to love and be creative human beings.

In this society, in the United States of America today, we are surrounded by the very wealth and the scientific achievements which hold forth a promise of freedom. Freedom is so near, yet at the same time it is so far away. And this thought invokes in me the same sensation I felt as I reflected on my own condition in a jail in New York City. For from my cell I could look down upon the crowded streets of

Greenwich Village, almost tasting the freedom of movement and the freedom of space which had been taken from me and all my sisters in captivity.

It was so near but at the same time so far away because somebody was holding the keys that would open the gates to freedom. Our condition here and now – the condition of all of us who are brown and black and working women and men – bears a very striking similarity to the condition of the prisoner. The wealth and the technology around us tells us that a free, humane, harmonious society lies very near. But at the same time it is so far away because someone is holding the keys and that someone refuses to open the gates to freedom. Like the prisoner we are locked up with the ugliness of racism and poverty and war and all the attendant mental frustrations and manipulations.

We're also locked up with our dreams and visions of freedom, and with the knowledge that if we only had the keys – if we could only seize them from the keepers, from the Standard Oils, the General Motors and all the giant corporations, and of course from their protectors, the government – if we could only get our hands on those keys we could transform these visions and these dreams into reality. [applause] Our situation bears a very excruciating similarity to the situation of the prisoner, and we must never forget this. For if we do, we will lose our desire for freedom and our will to struggle for liberation.

As black people, as brown people, as people of color, as working men and women in general, we know and we experience the agony of the struggle for existence each day. We are locked into that struggle. The parallels between our lives and the lives of our sisters and brothers behind bars are very clear. Yet there is a terrifying difference in degree between life on this side of the bars and life on the other side. And just as we must learn from the similarities and acquire an awareness of all the forces which oppress us out here, it is equally important that we understand that the plight of the prisoner unfolds in the rock-bottom realms of human existence.

Our sisters and brothers down there need our help, and our solidarity in their collective strivings and struggles in the same elemental way that we all need fresh air, and nourishment and shelter.

And when I say this I mean it to be taken quite literally, because I recall too well that in the bleak silence and solitude of a Marin County isolation cell, you, the people, were my only hope, my only promise of life.

Martin Luther King told us what he saw when he went to the mountaintop. He told us of visions of a new world of freedom and harmony; told us of the sisterhood and brotherhood of humankind. Doctor King described it far more eloquently than I could ever attempt to do. But there's also the foot of the mountain, and there are also the regions beneath the surface. And I am returning from a descent together with thousands and thousands of our sisters and brothers into the ugly depths of society. I want to try to tell you a little something about those regions. I want to attempt to persuade you to join in the struggle to give life and breath to those who live sealed away from everything that resembles human decency.

Listen for a moment to George Jackson's description of life in Soledad Prison's O- Wing: "This place destroys the logical processes of the mind. A man's thoughts become completely disorganized. The noise, madness streaming from every throat, frustrated sounds from the bars, metallic sounds from the walls, the steel trays, the iron beds bolted to the wall, the hollow sounds from a cast iron sink, a toilet, the smells, the human waste thrown at us, unwashed bodies, the rotten food. One can understand the depression felt by an inmate on max row. He's fallen as far as he can get into the social trap. Relief is so distant that it is very easy for him to lose his hopes. It's worse than Vietnam. And the guards with the carbines, and their sticks and tear gas are there to preserve this terror, to preserve it at any cost."

This in fact is what they told us at the trial in San Jose. I'd like to read a passage from our cross examination of one Sgt. Murphy, who was being questioned about San Quentin's policy about preventing escapes.

"Question: 'And to be certain I understand the significance of that policy, sir, does that policy mean that if people are attempting to escape, and if they have

hostages, and if the guards are able at all to prevent that escape, that they are to prevent that escape even if it means that every hostage is killed?

"Answer: That is correct.

"Question: And that means whether they're holding one judge or five judges, or one woman or twenty women, or one child or twenty children, that the policy of San Quentin guards is that at all costs they must prevent the escape. Is that right?

"Answer: That also includes the officers that work in the institution, sir.

"Question: Alright. Even if they are holding other officers who work in the institution, that should not deter the San Quentin correctional officers from preventing an escape at all costs. Is that right?

"Answer: That is correct.

"Question: In other words, it is more important to prevent the escape than to save human life. Is that correct?

Answer: Yes, sir." " ["Ooh! Right!" applause]

You can find this in the official court records of the trial. This Sgt. Murphy told us that day why San Quentin guards were so eager to pump their bullets into the bodies of Jonathan Jackson, William Christmas, James McClain, and Ruchell Magee even if it meant that a judge, a D.A., and women jurors might also be felled by their bullets. The terror of life in prison, its awesome presence in the society at large, could not be disturbed. Murphy called the prison by its rightful name. He captured the essence of the sociopolitical function of prisons today, for he was talking about a self-perpetuating system of terror. For prisons are political weapons; they function as means of containing elements in this society which threaten the stability of the larger system.

In prisons, people who are actually or potentially disruptive of the status quo are confined, contained, punished, and in some cases, forced to undergo psychological treatment by mind-altering drugs. This is happening in the state of California. The prison system is a weapon of repression. The government views young black and brown people as actually and potentially the most rebellious elements of this society. And thus the jails and prisons of this society are overflowing with young people of color. Anyone who has seen the streets of ghettos and barrios can already understand how easily a sister or a brother can fall victim to the police who are always there en masse.

Depending on the area, this country's prison population contains from 45 percent to 85 percent people of color. Nationally, 60 percent of all women prisoners are black. And tens of thousands of prisoners in city and county jails have never been convicted of any crime; they're simply there, victims – they're there under the control of insensitive, incompetent, and often blatantly racist public defenders who insist that they plead guilty even though they know that their client is just as innocent as they are. And for those who have committed a crime, we have to seek out the root cause. And we seek this cause not in them as individuals, but in the capitalist system that produces the need for crime in the first place.

As one student of the prisons system has said, "Thus the materially hungry must steal to survive, and the spiritually hungry commit anti-social acts because their human needs cannot be met in a property-oriented state. It is a fair estimate," he goes on to say, "that somewhere around 90 percent of the crimes committed would not be considered crimes or would not occur in a people-oriented society." In October 1970 a prisoner who had taken part in The Tombs rebellion in New York gave the following answers to questions put to him by a newsman.

"Question: 'What is your name? "Answer: I am a revolutionary.
"Question: What are you charged with? "Answer: I was born black.
"Question: How long have you been in?
"Answer: I've had trouble since the day I was born.' "

Once our sisters and brothers are entrapped inside these massive medieval fortresses and dungeons whether for nothing at all, or whether for frame-up political charges, whether for trying to escape their misery through a petty property crime, through narcotics or prostitution, they are caught in a vicious circle.

For if on the other side of the walls they try to continue or to begin to be men and women, the brutality they face, the brutality they must face, increases with mounting speed. I remember very well the women in the house of detention in New York who vowed to leave the heroin alone which was beginning to destroy their lives. Women who vowed to stand up and fight a system which had driven them to illusory escape through drugs. Women who began to outwardly exhibit their new commitment and their new transformation. And these were the women whom the worst of the matrons sought out, to punish them, and to put them in the hole.

George Jackson was murdered by mindless, carbine-toting San Quentin guards because he refused, he resisted, and he helped to teach his fellow prisoners that there was hope through struggle. And now in San Quentin – in San Quentin's Adjustment Center, which is a euphemistic term for the worst of the worst in prison – there are six more brothers who are facing charges of murder stemming from that day when George was killed. There was Fleeta Drumgo, who as a Soledad Brother was recently acquitted from similar frame-up charges. There are Hugo Pinell, Larry Spain, Luis Talamantez, David Johnson, and Willie Tate.

As I was saved and freed by the people so we must save and free these beautiful, struggling brothers. [applause] We must save them. And we must also save and free Ruchell Magee. And Wesley Robert Wells, who has spent over forty years of his life in California's prison system because he refused to submit, because he was a man. We must save, right here in southern California, Gary Lawton. And Geronimo Ortega, and Ricardo Chavez. And all of our sisters and brothers who must live with and struggle together against the terrible realities of captivity.

My freedom was achieved as the outcome of a massive, a massive people's struggle. Young people and older people, black, brown, Asian, Native American and white people, students and workers. The people seized the keys which opened the gates to freedom. And we've just begun. The momentum of this movement must be sustained, and it must be increased. Let us try to seize more keys and open more gates and bring out more sisters and brothers so that they can join the ranks of our struggle out here.

In building a prison movement, we must not forget our brothers who are suffering in military prisons and the stockades on bases throughout the country and across the globe. Let us not forget Billy Dean Smith. Billy Dean Smith, one of our black brothers who is now awaiting court-martial in Fort Ord, California. In Vietnam, this courageous brother from this city – from Watts, in fact, I think – would not follow orders. For he refused, he refused to murder the Vietnamese whom he knew as his comrades in the struggle for liberation. He would not follow orders. And of course in the eyes of his superior he was a very, very dangerous example to the other GI's. He had to be eliminated. So he was falsely accused with killing two white officers in Vietnam. In Biên Hòa, Vietnam. We must free Billy Dean Smith. We must free Billy Dean Smith and all his brothers and comrades who are imprisoned in the military.

We must be about the business of building a movement so strong and so powerful that it will not only free individuals like me – like the Soledad Brothers, the San Quentin Six, Billy Dean Smith – but one which will begin to attack the very foundations of the prison system itself.

And in doing this, the prison movement must be integrated into our struggles for black and brown liberation, and to our struggles for an end to material want and need. A very long struggle awaits us. And we know that it would be very romantic and idealistic to entertain immediate goals of tearing down all the walls of all the jails and prisons throughout this country. We should take on the task of freeing as many of our sisters and brothers as possible. And at the same time we must demand the ultimate abolition of the prison system along with the revolutionary transformation of this society. However, however, within the context of fighting for fundamental changes, there is something else we must do.

We must try to alter the very fabric of life behind walls as much as is possible through struggle, and there are a thousand concrete issues around which we can build this movement: uncensored and unlimited mail privileges, visits of the prisoners' choice, minimum wage levels in prison, adequate medical care – and for women this is particularly important when you consider that in some prisons a woman, a pregnant woman has to fight just to get one glass of milk per day. I saw this in New York. There are other issues. Literature must be uncensored. Prisoners must have the right to school themselves as they see fit. If they wish to learn about Marxism, Leninism, and about socialist revolution, then they should have the right to do it. This is their right and they should have the full flexibility to do so. There should be no more "kangaroo courts" behind prison walls. There should be no more kangaroo courts wherein one can be charged with a simple violation of prison regulations and end up spending the rest of one's life there simply because the parole board would have it that way. And there must be an end, there must be an end to the tormenting, indeterminate sentence policy with which a prisoner like George Jackson could be sentenced from one year to life after having been convicted of stealing a mere $75.

For if you talk to any prisoner in the state of California and in other states where the indeterminate sentence law prevails, they will inevitably say that this is the most grueling aspect of life in prison. Going before a board of ex-cops, ex- narcotics agents, ex-FBI agents, and ex-prison guards and year after year after year after year being told to wait it out until next time.

These are just a few of the issues that we are going to have to deal with. And all of them, every single one of them, is the kind of issue which any decent human being should be able to understand.

The need, the very urgent need to join our sisters and brothers behind bars in their struggle was brought home during the rebellion and the massacre at Attica last year. And I would like to close by reading a brief passage from a set of reflections I wrote in Marin County Jail upon hearing of the Attica revolt and massacre.

"The damage has been done, scores of men – some yet nameless – are dead. Unknown numbers are wounded. By now it would seem more people should realize that such explosions of repression are not isolated aberrations in a society not terribly disturbing. For we have witnessed Birmingham and Orangeburg, Jackson State, Kent State, My Lai and San Quentin August 21. The list is unending.

"None of these explosions emerged out of nothing. Rather, they all crystallized and attested to profound and extensive social infirmities.

"But Attica was different from these other episodes in one very important respect. For this time the authorities were indicted by the very events themselves; they were caught red-handed in their lies.

They were publicly exposed when to justify that massacre – a massacre which was led by Governor Rockefeller and agreed to by President Nixon – when they hastened to falsify what had occurred.

"Perhaps this in itself has pulled greater numbers of people from their socially- inflicted slumber. Many have already expressed outrage, but outrage is not enough. Governments and prison bureaucracies must be subjected to fears and unqualified criticism for their harsh and murderous repression. But even this is not enough, for this is not yet the root of the matter. People must take a forthright stand in active support of prisoners and their grievances. They must try to comprehend the

eminently human content of prisoners' stirrings and struggles. For it is justice that we seek, and many of us can already envision a world unblemished by poverty and alienation, one where the prison would be but a vague memory, a relic of the past.

"But we also have immediate demands for justice right now, for fairness, and for room to think and live and act."

Thank you.

THINK
EDUCATION

Martin Luther King, Jr.

Beyond Vietnam -- A Time to Break Silence

Delivered 4 April 1967, Riverside Church, New York City

Mr. Chairman, ladies and gentlemen:

I need not pause to say how very delighted I am to be here tonight, and how very delighted I am to see you expressing your concern about the issues that will be discussed tonight by turning out in such large numbers. I also want to say that I consider it a great honor to share this program with Dr. Bennett, Dr. Commager, and Rabbi Heschel, and some of the distinguished leaders and personalities of our nation. And of course it's always good to come back to Riverside church. Over the last eight years, I have had the privilege of preaching here almost every year in that period, and it is always a rich and rewarding experience to come to this great church and this great pulpit.

I come to this magnificent house of worship tonight because my conscience leaves me no other choice. I join you in this meeting because I'm in deepest agreement with the aims and work of the organization which has brought us together: Clergy and Laymen Concerned About Vietnam. The recent statements of your executive committee are the sentiments of my own heart, and I found myself in full accord when I read its opening lines: "A time comes when silence is betrayal." And that time has come for us in relation to Vietnam.

The truth of these words is beyond doubt, but the mission to which they call us is a most difficult one. Even when pressed by the demands of inner truth, men do not easily assume the task of opposing their government's policy, especially in time of war. Nor does the human spirit move without great difficulty against all the apathy of conformist thought within one's own bosom and in the surrounding world.
Moreover, when the issues at hand seem as perplexing as they often do in the case of this dreadful conflict, we are always on the verge of being mesmerized by uncertainty; but we must move on.

And some of us who have already begun to break the silence of the night have found that the calling to speak is often a vocation of agony, but we must speak. We must speak with all the humility that is appropriate to our limited vision, but we must speak. And we must rejoice as well, for surely this is the first time in our nation's history that a significant number of its religious leaders have chosen to move beyond the prophesying of smooth patriotism to the high grounds of a firm dissent based upon the mandates of conscience and the reading of history. Perhaps a new spirit is rising among us. If it is, let us trace its movements and pray that our own inner being may be sensitive to its guidance, for we are deeply in need of a new way beyond the darkness that seems so close around us.

Over the past two years, as I have moved to break the betrayal of my own silences and to speak from the burnings of my own heart, as I have called for radical departures from the destruction of Vietnam, many persons have questioned me about the wisdom of my path. At the heart of their concerns this query has often loomed large and loud: "Why are you speaking about the war, Dr. King?" "Why are

you joining the voices of dissent?" "Peace and civil rights don't mix," they say. "Aren't you hurting the cause of your people," they ask? And when I hear them, though I often understand the source of their concern, I am nevertheless greatly saddened, for such questions mean that the inquirers have not really known me, my commitment or my calling. Indeed, their questions suggest that they do not know the world in which they live.

In the light of such tragic misunderstanding, I deem it of signal importance to try to state clearly, and I trust concisely, why I believe that the path from Dexter Avenue Baptist Church -- the church in Montgomery, Alabama, where I began my pastorate -- leads clearly to this sanctuary tonight.

I come to this platform tonight to make a passionate plea to my beloved nation. This speech is not addressed to Hanoi or to the National Liberation Front. It is not addressed to China or to Russia. Nor is it an attempt to overlook the ambiguity of the total situation and the need for a collective solution to the tragedy of Vietnam. Neither is it an attempt to make North Vietnam or the National Liberation Front paragons of virtue, nor to overlook the role they must play in the successful resolution of the problem. While they both may have justifiable reasons to be suspicious of the good faith of the United States, life and history give eloquent testimony to the fact that conflicts are never resolved without trustful give and take on both sides.

Tonight, however, I wish not to speak with Hanoi and the National

Liberation Front, but rather to my fellow Americans.

Since I am a preacher by calling, I suppose it is not surprising that I have seven major reasons for bringing Vietnam into the field of my moral vision. There is at the outset a very obvious and almost facile connection between the war in Vietnam and the struggle I, and others, have been waging in America. A few years ago there was a shining moment in that struggle. It seemed as if there was a real promise of hope for the poor -- both black and white -- through the poverty program. There were experiments, hopes, new beginnings. Then came the buildup in Vietnam, and I

watched this program broken and eviscerated, as if it were some idle political plaything of a society gone mad on war, and I knew that America would never invest the necessary funds or energies in rehabilitation of its poor so long as adventures like Vietnam continued to draw men and skills and money like some demonic destructive suction tube. So, I was increasingly compelled to see the war as an enemy of the poor and to attack it as such.

Perhaps a more tragic recognition of reality took place when it became clear to me that the war was doing far more than devastating the hopes of the poor at home. It was sending their sons and their brothers and their husbands to fight and to die in extraordinarily high proportions relative to the rest of the population. We were taking the black young men who had been crippled by our society and sending them eight thousand miles away to guarantee liberties in Southeast Asia which they had not found in southwest Georgia and East Harlem. And so we have been repeatedly faced with the cruel irony of watching Negro and white boys on TV screens as they kill and die together for a nation that has been unable to seat them together in the same schools. And so we watch them in brutal solidarity burning the huts of a poor village, but we realize that they would hardly live on the same block in Chicago. I could not be silent in the face of such cruel manipulation of the poor.

My third reason moves to an even deeper level of awareness, for it grows out of my experience in the ghettoes of the North over the last three years -- especially the last three summers. As I have walked among the desperate, rejected, and angry young men, I have told them that Molotov cocktails and rifles would not solve their problems. I have tried to offer them my deepest compassion while maintaining my conviction that social change comes most meaningfully through nonviolent action.

But they ask -- and rightly so -- what about Vietnam? They ask if our own nation wasn't using massive doses of violence to solve its problems, to bring about the changes it wanted. Their questions hit home, and I knew that I could never again raise my voice against the violence of the oppressed in the ghettos without having first spoken clearly to the greatest purveyor of violence in the world today -- my own government. For the sake of those boys, for the sake of this government, for

the sake of the hundreds of thousands trembling under our violence, I cannot be silent.

For those who ask the question, "Aren't you a civil rights leader?" and thereby mean to exclude me from the movement for peace, I have this further answer. In 1957 when a group of us formed the Southern Christian Leadership Conference, we chose as our motto: "To save the soul of America." We were convinced that we could not limit our vision to certain rights for black people, but instead affirmed the conviction that America would never be free or saved from itself until the descendants of its slaves were loosed completely from the shackles they still wear. In a way we were agreeing with Langston Hughes, that black bard of Harlem, who had written earlier:

O, yes,
I say it plain,
America never was America to me, And yet I swear this oath --
America will be!

Now, it should be incandescently clear that no one who has any concern for the integrity and life of America today can ignore the present war. If America's soul becomes totally poisoned, part of the autopsy must read: Vietnam. It can never be saved so long as it destroys the deepest hopes of men the world over. So it is that those of us who are yet determined that America will be -- are -- are led down the path of protest and dissent, working for the health of our land.

As if the weight of such a commitment to the life and health of America were not enough, another burden of responsibility was placed upon me in 1954;1 and I cannot forget that the Nobel Peace Prize was also a commission, a commission to work harder than I had ever worked before for "the brotherhood of man." This is a calling that takes me beyond national allegiances, but even if it were not present I would yet have to live with the meaning of my commitment to the ministry of Jesus Christ. To me the relationship of this ministry to the making of peace is so obvious

that I sometimes marvel at those who ask me why I'm speaking against the war. Could it be that they do not know that the good news was meant for all men -- for Communist and capitalist, for their children and ours, for black and for white, for revolutionary and conservative? Have they forgotten that my ministry is in obedience to the One who loved his enemies so fully that he died for them? What then can I say to the Vietcong or to Castro or to Mao as a faithful minister of this One? Can I threaten them with death or must I not share with them my life?

And finally, as I try to explain for you and for myself the road that leads from Montgomery to this place I would have offered all that was most valid if I simply said that I must be true to my conviction that I share with all men the calling to be a son of the living God. Beyond the calling of race or nation or creed is this vocation of sonship and brotherhood, and because I believe that the Father is deeply concerned especially for his suffering and helpless and outcast children, I come tonight to speak for them.

This I believe to be the privilege and the burden of all of us who deem ourselves bound by allegiances and loyalties which are broader and deeper than nationalism and which go beyond our nation's self-defined goals and positions. We are called to speak for the weak, for the voiceless, for the victims of our nation and for those it calls "enemy," for no document from human hands can make these humans any less our brothers.

And as I ponder the madness of Vietnam and search within myself for ways to understand and respond in compassion, my mind goes constantly to the people of that peninsula. I speak now not of the soldiers of each side, not of the ideologies of the Liberation Front, not of the junta in Saigon, but simply of the people who have been living under the curse of war for almost three continuous decades now.

I think of them, too, because it is clear to me that there will be no meaningful solution there until some attempt is made to know them and hear their broken cries.

They must see Americans as strange liberators. The Vietnamese people proclaimed

their own independence in 1954 -- in 1945 rather -- after a combined French and Japanese occupation and before the communist revolution in China. They were led by Ho Chi Minh. Even though they quoted the American Declaration of Independence in their own document of freedom, we refused to recognize them. Instead, we decided to support France in its reconquest of her former colony. Our government felt then that the Vietnamese people were not ready for independence, and we again fell victim to the deadly Western arrogance that has poisoned the international atmosphere for so long. With that tragic decision we rejected a revolutionary government seeking self-determination and a government that had been established not by China -- for whom the Vietnamese have no great love -- but by clearly indigenous forces that included some communists. For the peasants this new government meant real land reform, one of the most important needs in their lives.

For nine years following 1945 we denied the people of Vietnam the right of independence. For nine years we vigorously supported the French in their abortive effort to recolonize Vietnam. Before the end of the war we were meeting eighty percent of the French war costs. Even before the French were defeated at Dien Bien Phu, they began to despair of their reckless action, but we did not. We encouraged them with our huge financial and military supplies to continue the war even after they had lost the will. Soon we would be paying almost the full costs of this tragic attempt at recolonization.

After the French were defeated, it looked as if independence and land reform would come again through the Geneva Agreement. But instead there came the United States, determined that Ho should not unify the temporarily divided nation, and the peasants watched again as we supported one of the most vicious modern dictators, our chosen man, Premier Diem. The peasants watched and cringed as Diem ruthlessly rooted out all opposition, supported their extortionist landlords, and refused even to discuss reunification with the North.

The peasants watched as all this was presided over by United States' influence and then by increasing numbers of United States troops who came to help quell the insurgency that Diem's methods had aroused. When Diem was overthrown they may have been

happy, but the long line of military dictators seemed to offer no real change, especially in terms of their need for land and peace.

The only change came from America, as we increased our troop commitments in support of governments which were singularly corrupt, inept, and without popular support. All the while the people read our leaflets and received the regular promises of peace and democracy and land reform. Now they languish under our bombs and consider us, not their fellow Vietnamese, the real enemy. They move sadly and apathetically as we herd them off the land of their fathers into concentration camps where minimal social needs are rarely met. They know they must move on or be destroyed by our bombs.

So they go, primarily women and children and the aged. They watch as we poison their water, as we kill a million acres of their crops. They must weep as the bulldozers roar through their areas preparing to destroy the precious trees. They wander into the hospitals with at least twenty casualties from American firepower for one Vietcong-inflicted injury. So far we may have killed a million of them, mostly children. They wander into the towns and see thousands of the children, homeless, without clothes, running in packs on the streets like animals. They see the children degraded by our soldiers as they beg for food. They see the children selling their sisters to our soldiers, soliciting for their mothers.

What do the peasants think as we ally ourselves with the landlords and as we refuse to put any action into our many words concerning land reform? What do they think as we test out our latest weapons on them, just as the Germans tested out new medicine and new tortures in the concentration camps of Europe? Where are the roots of the independent Vietnam we claim to be building? Is it among these voiceless ones?

We have destroyed their two most cherished institutions: the family and the village. We have destroyed their land and their crops. We have cooperated in the crushing -- in the crushing of the nation's only non-Communist revolutionary political force, the unified Buddhist Church. We have supported the enemies of the

peasants of Saigon. We have corrupted their women and children and killed their men.

Now there is little left to build on, save bitterness. Soon, the only solid -- solid physical foundations remaining will be found at our military bases and in the concrete of the concentration camps we call "fortified hamlets." The peasants may well wonder if we plan to build our new Vietnam on such grounds as these. Could we blame them for such thoughts? We must speak for them and raise the questions they cannot raise. These, too, are our brothers.

Perhaps a more difficult but no less necessary task is to speak for those who have been designated as our enemies. What of the National Liberation Front, that strangely anonymous group we call "VC" or "communists"? What must they think of the United States of America when they realize that we permitted the repression and cruelty of Diem, which helped to bring them into being as a resistance group in the South? What do they think of our condoning the violence which led to their own taking up of arms? How can they believe in our integrity when now we speak of "aggression from the North" as if there were nothing more essential to the war?
How can they trust us when now we charge them with violence after the murderous reign of Diem and charge them with violence while we pour every new weapon of death into their land? Surely we must understand their feelings, even if we do not condone their actions. Surely we must see that the men we supported pressed them to their violence. Surely we must see that our own computerized plans of destruction simply dwarf their greatest acts.

How do they judge us when our officials know that their membership is less than twenty-five percent communist, and yet insist on giving them the blanket name? What must they be thinking when they know that we are aware of their control of major sections of Vietnam, and yet we appear ready to allow national elections in which this highly organized political parallel government will not have a part? They ask how we can speak of free elections when the Saigon press is censored and controlled by the military junta. And they are surely right to wonder what kind of new government we plan to help form without them, the only party in real touch

with the peasants. They question our political goals and they deny the reality of a peace settlement from which they will be excluded. Their questions are frighteningly relevant. Is our nation planning to build on political myth again, and then shore it up upon the power of new violence?

Here is the true meaning and value of compassion and nonviolence, when it helps us to see the enemy's point of view, to hear his questions, to know his assessment of ourselves. For from his view we may indeed see the basic weaknesses of our own condition, and if we are mature, we may learn and grow and profit from the wisdom of the brothers who are called the opposition.

So, too, with Hanoi. In the North, where our bombs now pummel the land, and our mines endanger the waterways, we are met by a deep but understandable mistrust. To speak for them is to explain this lack of confidence in Western words, and especially their distrust of American intentions now. In Hanoi are the men who led the nation to independence against the Japanese and the French, the men who sought membership in the French Commonwealth and were betrayed by the weakness of Paris and the willfulness of the colonial armies. It was they who led a second struggle against French domination at tremendous costs, and then were persuaded to give up the land they controlled between the thirteenth and seventeenth parallel as a temporary measure at Geneva. After 1954 they watched us conspire with Diem to prevent elections which could have surely brought Ho Chi Minh to power over a united Vietnam, and they realized they had been betrayed again. When we ask why they do not leap to negotiate, these things must be remembered.

Also, it must be clear that the leaders of Hanoi considered the presence of American troops in support of the Diem regime to have been the initial military breach of the Geneva Agreement concerning foreign troops. They remind us that they did not begin to send troops in large numbers and even supplies into the South until American forces had moved into the tens of thousands.

Hanoi remembers how our leaders refused to tell us the truth about the earlier North Vietnamese overtures for peace, how the president claimed that none existed when they had clearly been made. Ho Chi Minh has watched as America has spoken of peace and built up its forces, and now he has surely heard the increasing international rumors of American plans for an invasion of the North. He knows the bombing and shelling and mining we are doing are part of traditional pre-invasion strategy. Perhaps only his sense of humor and of irony can save him when he hears the most powerful nation of the world speaking of aggression as it drops thousands of bombs on a poor, weak nation more than eight hundred -- rather, eight thousand miles away from its shores.

At this point I should make it clear that while I have tried in these last few minutes to give a voice to the voiceless in Vietnam and to understand the arguments of those who are called "enemy," I am as deeply concerned about our own troops there as anything else. For it occurs to me that what we are submitting them to in Vietnam is not simply the brutalizing process that goes on in any war where armies face each other and seek to destroy. We are adding cynicism to the process of death, for they must know after a short period there that none of the things we claim to be fighting for are really involved. Before long they must know that their government has sent them into a struggle among Vietnamese, and the more sophisticated surely realize that we are on the side of the wealthy, and the secure, while we create a hell for the poor.

Somehow this madness must cease. We must stop now. I speak as a child of God and brother to the suffering poor of Vietnam. I speak for those whose land is being laid waste, whose homes are being destroyed, whose culture is being subverted. I speak of the -- for the poor of America who are paying the double price of smashed hopes at home, and death and corruption in Vietnam. I speak as a citizen of the world, for the world as it stands aghast at the path we have taken. I speak as one who loves America, to the leaders of our own nation: The great initiative in this war is ours; the initiative to stop it must be ours.

This is the message of the great Buddhist leaders of Vietnam. Recently one of them wrote these words, and I quote:

Each day the war goes on the hatred increases in the heart of the Vietnamese and in the hearts of those of humanitarian instinct. The

Americans are forcing even their friends into becoming their enemies. It is curious that the Americans, who calculate so carefully on the possibilities of military victory, do not realize that in the process they are incurring deep psychological and political defeat. The image of America will never again be the image of revolution, freedom, and democracy, but the image of violence and militarism (unquote).

If we continue, there will be no doubt in my mind and in the mind of the world that we have no honorable intentions in Vietnam. If we do not stop our war against the people of Vietnam immediately, the world will be left with no other alternative than to see this as some horrible, clumsy, and deadly game we have decided to play. The world now demands a maturity of America that we may not be able to achieve. It demands that we admit that we have been wrong from the beginning of our adventure in Vietnam, that we have been detrimental to the life of the Vietnamese people. The situation is one in which we must be ready to turn sharply from our present ways. In order to atone for our sins and errors in Vietnam, we should take the initiative in bringing a halt to this tragic war.

I would like to suggest five concrete things that our government should do [immediately] to begin the long and difficult process of extricating ourselves from this nightmarish conflict:

Number one: End all bombing in North and South Vietnam.

Number two: Declare a unilateral cease-fire in the hope that such action will create the atmosphere for negotiation.

Three: Take immediate steps to prevent other battlegrounds in Southeast Asia by curtailing our military buildup in Thailand and our interference in Laos.

Four: Realistically accept the fact that the National Liberation Front has substantial support in South Vietnam and must thereby play a role in any meaningful negotiations and any future Vietnam government.

Five: Set a date that we will remove all foreign troops from Vietnam in accordance with the 1954 Geneva Agreement.

Part of our ongoing -- Part of our ongoing commitment might well express itself in an offer to grant asylum to any Vietnamese who fears for his life under a new regime which included the Liberation Front. Then we must make what reparations we can for the damage we have done. We must provide the medical aid that is badly needed, making it available in this country, if necessary. Meanwhile -- Meanwhile, we in the churches and synagogues have a continuing task while we urge our government to disengage itself from a disgraceful commitment. We must continue to raise our voices and our lives if our nation persists in its perverse ways in Vietnam. We must be prepared to match actions with words by seeking out every creative method of protest possible.

As we counsel young men concerning military service, we must clarify for them our nation's role in Vietnam and challenge them with the alternative of conscientious objection. I am pleased to say that this is a path now chosen by more than seventy students at my own alma mater, Morehouse College, and I recommend it to all who find the American course in Vietnam a dishonorable and unjust one. Moreover, I would encourage all ministers of draft age to give up their ministerial exemptions and seek status as conscientious objectors. These are the times for real choices and not false ones. We are at the moment when our lives must be placed on the line if our nation is to survive its own folly. Every man of humane convictions must decide on the protest that best suits his convictions, but we must all protest.

Now there is something seductively tempting about stopping there and sending us all off on what in some circles has become a popular crusade against the war in Vietnam. I say we must enter that struggle, but I wish to go on now to say

something even more disturbing.

The war in Vietnam is but a symptom of a far deeper malady within the American spirit, and if we ignore this sobering reality...and if we ignore this sobering reality, we will find ourselves organizing "clergy and laymen concerned" committees for the next generation. They will be concerned about Guatemala -- Guatemala and Peru. They will be concerned about Thailand and Cambodia. They will be concerned about Mozambique and South Africa. We will be marching for these and a dozen other names and attending rallies without end, unless there is a significant and profound change in American life and policy.

And so, such thoughts take us beyond Vietnam, but not beyond our calling as sons of the living God.

In 1957, a sensitive American official overseas said that it seemed to him that our nation was on the wrong side of a world revolution. During the past ten years, we have seen emerge a pattern of suppression which has now justified the presence of U.S. military advisors in Venezuela. This need to maintain social stability for our investments accounts for the counterrevolutionary action of American forces in Guatemala. It tells why American helicopters are being used against guerrillas in Cambodia and why American napalm and Green Beret forces have already been active against rebels in Peru.

It is with such activity in mind that the words of the late John F. Kennedy come back to haunt us. Five years ago he said, "Those who make peaceful revolution impossible will make violent revolution inevitable." Increasingly, by choice or by accident, this is the role our nation has taken, the role of those who make peaceful revolution impossible by refusing to give up the privileges and the pleasures that come from the immense profits of overseas investments. I am convinced that if we are to get on the right side of the world revolution, we as a nation must undergo a radical revolution of values. We must rapidly begin...we must rapidly begin the shift from a thing-oriented society to a person-oriented society. When machines and computers, profit motives and property rights, are considered more important than

people, the giant triplets of racism, extreme materialism, and militarism are incapable of being conquered.

A true revolution of values will soon cause us to question the fairness and justice of many of our past and present policies. On the one hand, we are called to play the Good Samaritan on life's roadside, but that will be only an initial act. One day we must come to see that the whole Jericho Road must be transformed so that men and women will not be constantly beaten and robbed as they make their journey on life's highway. True compassion is more than flinging a coin to a beggar. It comes to see that an edifice which produces beggars needs restructuring.

A true revolution of values will soon look uneasily on the glaring contrast of poverty and wealth. With righteous indignation, it will look across the seas and see individual capitalists of the West investing huge sums of money in Asia, Africa, and South America, only to take the profits out with no concern for the social betterment of the countries, and say, "This is not just." It will look at our alliance with the landed gentry of South America and say, "This is not just." The Western arrogance of feeling that it has everything to teach others and nothing to learn from them is not just.

A true revolution of values will lay hand on the world order and say of war, "This way of settling differences is not just." This business of burning human beings with napalm, of filling our nation's homes with orphans and widows, of injecting poisonous drugs of hate into the veins of peoples normally humane, of sending men home from dark and bloody battlefields physically handicapped and psychologically deranged, cannot be reconciled with wisdom, justice, and love. A nation that continues year after year to spend more money on military defense than on programs of social uplift is approaching spiritual death.

America, the richest and most powerful nation in the world, can well lead the way in this revolution of values. There is nothing except a tragic death wish to prevent us from reordering our priorities so that the pursuit of peace will take precedence

over the pursuit of war. There is nothing to keep us from molding a recalcitrant status quo with bruised hands until we have fashioned it into a brotherhood.

This kind of positive revolution of values is our best defense against communism. War is not the answer. Communism will never be defeated by the use of atomic bombs or nuclear weapons. Let us not join those who shout war and, through their misguided passions, urge the United States to relinquish its participation in the United Nations. These are days which demand wise restraint and calm reasonableness. We must not engage in a negative anticommunism, but rather in a positive thrust for democracy, realizing that our greatest defense against communism is to take offensive action in behalf of justice. We must with positive action seek to remove those conditions of poverty, insecurity, and injustice, which are the fertile soil in which the seed of communism grows and develops.

These are revolutionary times. All over the globe men are revolting against old systems of exploitation and oppression, and out of the wounds of a frail world, new systems of justice and equality are being born. The shirtless and barefoot people of the land are rising up as never before. "The people who sat in darkness have seen a great light."2 We in the West must support these revolutions.

It is a sad fact that because of comfort, complacency, a morbid fear of communism, and our proneness to adjust to injustice, the Western nations that initiated so much of the revolutionary spirit of the modern world have now become the arch antirevolutionaries. This has driven many to feel that only Marxism has a revolutionary spirit. Therefore, communism is a judgment against our failure to make democracy real and follow through on the revolutions that we initiated. Our only hope today lies in our ability to recapture the revolutionary spirit and go out into a sometimes hostile world declaring eternal hostility to poverty, racism, and militarism. With this powerful commitment we shall boldly challenge the status quo and unjust mores, and thereby speed the day when "every valley shall be exalted, and every mountain and hill shall be made low, and the crooked shall be made straight, and the rough places plain."3

A genuine revolution of values means in the final analysis that our loyalties must become ecumenical rather than sectional. Every nation must now develop an overriding loyalty to mankind as a whole in order to preserve the best in their individual societies.

This call for a worldwide fellowship that lifts neighborly concern beyond one's tribe, race, class, and nation is in reality a call for an all-embracing -- embracing and unconditional love for all mankind. This oft misunderstood, this oft misinterpreted concept, so readily dismissed by the Nietzsches of the world as a weak and cowardly force, has now become an absolute necessity for the survival of man. When I speak of love I am not speaking of some sentimental and weak response. I am not speaking of that force which is just emotional bosh. I am speaking of that force which all of the great religions have seen as the supreme unifying principle of life. Love is somehow the key that unlocks the door which leads to ultimate reality. This Hindu-Muslim-Christian-Jewish-Buddhist belief about ultimate -- ultimate reality is beautifully summed up in the first epistle of Saint John: "Let us love one another, for love is God. And every one that loveth is born of God and knoweth God. He that loveth not knoweth not God, for God is love." "If we love one another, God dwelleth in us and his love is perfected in us."4 Let us hope that this spirit will become the order of the day.

We can no longer afford to worship the god of hate or bow before the altar of retaliation. The oceans of history are made turbulent by the ever-rising tides of hate. And history is cluttered with the wreckage of nations and individuals that pursued this self-defeating path of hate. As Arnold Toynbee says:

Love is the ultimate force that makes for the saving choice of life and good against the damning choice of death and evil. Therefore the first hope in our inventory must be the hope that love is going to have the last word (unquote).

We are now faced with the fact, my friends that tomorrow is today. We are confronted with the fierce urgency of now. In this unfolding conundrum of life and history, there is such a thing as being too late. Procrastination is still the thief of

time. Life often leaves us standing bare, naked, and dejected with a lost opportunity. The tide in the affairs of men does not remain at flood -- it ebbs. We may cry out desperately for time to pause in her passage, but time is adamant to every plea and rushes on. Over the bleached bones and jumbled residues of numerous civilizations are written the pathetic words, "Too late." There is an invisible book of life that faithfully records our vigilance or our neglect. Omar Khayyam is right: "The moving finger writes, and having writ moves on."

We still have a choice today: nonviolent coexistence or violent co annihilation. We must move past indecision to action. We must find new ways to speak for peace in Vietnam and justice throughout the developing world, a world that borders on our doors. If we do not act, we shall surely be dragged down the long, dark, and shameful corridors of time reserved for those who possess power without compassion, might without morality, and strength without sight.

Now let us begin. Now let us rededicate ourselves to the long and bitter, but beautiful, struggle for a new world. This is the calling of the sons of God, and our brothers wait eagerly for our response. Shall we say the odds are too great? Shall we tell them the struggle is too hard? Will our message be that the forces of American life militate against their arrival as full men, and we send our deepest regrets? Or will there be another message -- of longing, of hope, of solidarity with their yearnings, of commitment to their cause, whatever the cost? The choice is ours, and though we might prefer it otherwise, we must choose in this crucial moment of human history.

As that noble bard of yesterday, James Russell Lowell, eloquently stated:

Once to every man and nation comes a moment to decide,
In the strife of truth and Falsehood, for the good or evil side;
Some great cause, God's new Messiah offering each the bloom or blight, And the choice goes by forever 'twixt that darkness and that light.
Though the cause of evil prosper, yet 'tis truth alone is strong though her portions be the scaffold, and upon the throne be wrong

yet that scaffold sways the future, and behind the dim unknown Standeth God within the shadow, keeping watch above his own.

And if we will only make the right choice, we will be able to transform this pending cosmic elegy into a creative psalm of peace. If we will make the right choice, we will be able to transform the jangling discords of our world into a beautiful symphony of brotherhood. If we will but make the right choice, we will be able to speed up the day, all over America and all over the world, when "justice will roll down like waters, and righteousness like a mighty stream."

Ida B. Wells,
"This Awful Slaughter" (1909)

By 1909 Ida B. Wells was the most prominent anti-lynching campaigner in the United States. From the early 1890s she labored mostly alone in her effort to raise the nation's awareness and indignation about these usually unpunished murders. In 1909, however, she gained a powerful ally in the newly formed National Association for the Advancement of Colored People (NAACP). The follow speech was delivered by Wells on May 8, 1909 at the NAACP's first annual conference held in Atlanta, Georgia.

The lynching record for a quarter of a century merits the thoughtful study of the American people. It presents three salient facts: First, lynching is color-line murder. Second, crimes against women is the excuse, not the cause. Third, it is a national crime and requires a national remedy. Proof that lynching follows the color line is to be found in the statistics which have been kept for the past twenty-five years. During the few years preceding this period and while frontier law existed, the executions showed a majority of white victims. Later, however, as law courts and authorized judiciary extended into the far West, lynch law rapidly abated, and its white victims became few and far between. Just as the lynch-law regime came to a close in the West, a new mob movement started in the South.

This was wholly political, its purpose being to suppress the colored vote by intimidation and murder. Thousands of assassins banded together under the name of Ku Klux Klans, "Midnight Raiders," "Knights of the Golden Circle," et cetera, et cetera, spread a reign of terror, by beating, shooting and killing colored in a few years, the purpose was accomplished, and the black vote was suppressed. But mob murder continued. From 1882, in which year fifty-two were lynched, down to the present, lynching has been along the color line. Mob murder increased yearly until in 1892 more than two hundred victims were lynched and statistics show that 3,284 men, women and children have been put to death in this quarter of a century. During the last ten years from 1899 to 1908 inclusive the number lynched was 959. Of this number 102 were white, while the colored victims numbered 857. No other nation, civilized or savage, burns its criminals; only under that Stars and Stripes is the human holocaust possible. Twenty-eight human beings burned at the stake, one of them a woman and two of them children, is the awful indictment against American civilization—the gruesome tribute which the nation pays to the color line.

Why is mob murder permitted by a Christian nation? What is the cause of this awful slaughter? This question is answered almost daily— always the same shameless falsehood that "Negroes are lynched to protect womanhood." Standing before a Chautauqua assemblage, John Temple Graves, at once champion of lynching and apologist for lynchers, said: "The mob stands today as the most potential bulwark between the women of the South and such a carnival of crime as would infuriate the world and precipitate the annihilation of the Negro race." This is the never-varying answer of lynchers and their apologists. All know that it is untrue. The cowardly lyncher revels in murder, then seeks to shield himself from public execration by claiming devotion to woman. But truth is mighty and the lynching record discloses the hypocrisy of the lyncher as well as his crime.

The Springfield, Illinois, mob rioted for two days, the militia of the entire state was called out, two men were lynched, hundreds of people driven from their homes, all because a white woman said a Negro assaulted her. A mad mob went to the jail, tried to lynch the victim of her charge and, not being able to find him, proceeded to pillage and burn the town and to lynch two innocent men. Later, after the police had found that the woman's charge was false, she published a retraction, the indictment was dismissed and the intended victim discharged. But the lynched victims were dead. Hundreds were homeless and Illinois was disgraced.

As a final and complete refutation of the charge that lynching is occasioned by crimes against women, a partial record of lynching's is cited; 285 persons were lynched for causes as follows: Unknown cause, 92; no cause, 10; race prejudice, 49; miscegenation, 7; informing, 12; making threats, 11; keeping saloon, 3; practicing fraud, 5; practicing voodooism, 1; refusing evidence, 2; political causes, 5; disputing, 1; disobeying quarantine regulations, 2; slapping a child, 1; turning state's evidence, 3; protecting a Negro, 1; to prevent giving evidence, 1; knowledge of larceny, 1; writing letter to white woman, 1; asking white woman to marry; 1; jilting girl, 1; having smallpox, 1; concealing criminal, 2; threatening political exposure, 1; self- defense, 6; cruelty; 1; insulting language to woman, 5; quarreling with white man, 2; colonizing Negroes, 1; throwing stones, 1; quarreling, 1; gambling, 1.

Is there a remedy, or will the nation confesses that it cannot protect its protectors at home as well as abroad? Various remedies have been suggested to abolish the lynching infamy, but year after year, the butchery of men, women and children continues in spite of plea and protest. Education is suggested as a preventive, but it is as grave a crime to murder an ignorant man as it is a scholar. True, few educated men have been lynched, but the hue and cry once started stops at no bounds, as was clearly shown by the lynching's in Atlanta, and in Springfield, Illinois.

Agitation, though helpful, will not alone stop the crime. Year after year statistics are published, meetings are held, resolutions are adopted and yet lynching's go on. Public sentiment does measurably decrease the sway of mob law, but the irresponsible bloodthirsty criminals who swept through the streets of Springfield, beating an inoffensive law-abiding citizen to death in one part of the town, and in another torturing and shooting to death a man who for threescore years had made a reputation for honesty; integrity and sobriety, had raised a family and had accumulated property; were not deterred from their heinous crimes by either education or agitation.

The only certain remedy is an appeal to law. Lawbreakers must be made to know that human life is sacred and that every citizen of this country is first a citizen of the United States and secondly a citizen of the state in which he belongs. This nation must assert itself and protect its federal citizenship at home as well as abroad. The strong arm of the government must reach across state lines whenever unbridled lawlessness defies state laws and must give to the individual under the Stars and Stripes the same measure of protection it gives to him when he travels in foreign lands.

Federal protection of American citizenship is the remedy for lynching. Foreigners are rarely lynched in America. If, by mistake, one is lynched, the national government quickly pays the damages. The recent agitation in California against the Japanese compelled this nation to recognize that federal power must yet assert itself to protect the nation from the treason of sovereign states. Thousands of American citizens have been put to death and no President has yet raised his hand in effective protest, but a simple insult to a native of Japan was quite sufficient to stir the government at Washington to prevent the threatened wrong. If the government has power to protect a foreigner from insult, certainly it has power to save a citizen's life.

The practical remedy has been more than once suggested in Congress. Senator Gallinger, of New Hampshire, in a resolution introduced in Congress called for an investigation "with the view of ascertaining whether there is a remedy for lynching which Congress may apply." The Senate Committee has under consideration a bill drawn by A. E. Pillsbury, formerly Attorney General of Massachusetts, providing for federal prosecution of lynchers in cases where the state fails to protect citizens or foreigners. Both of these resolutions indicate that the attention of the nation has been called to this phase of the lynching question.

As a final word, it would be a beginning in the right direction if this conference can see its way clear to establish a bureau for the investigation and publication of the details of every lynching, so that the public could know that an influential body of citizens has made it a duty to give the widest publicity to the facts in each case; that it will make an effort to secure expressions of opinion all over the country against lynching for the sake of the country's fair name; and lastly, but by no means least, to try to influence the daily papers of the country to refuse to become accessory to mobs either before or after the fact.

Several of the greatest riots and most brutal burnt offerings of the mobs have been suggested and incited by the daily papers of the offending community. If the newspaper which suggests lynching in its accounts of an alleged crime, could be held legally as well as morally responsible for reporting that "threats of lynching were heard"; or, "it is feared that if the guilty one is caught, he will be lynched"; or, "there were cries of 'lynch him,' and the only reason the threat was not carried out was because no leader appeared," a long step toward a remedy will have been taken.

In a multitude of counsel there is wisdom. Upon the grave question presented by the slaughter of innocent men, women and children there should be an honest, courageous conference of patriotic, law-abiding citizens anxious to punish crime promptly, impartially and by due process of law, also to make life, liberty and property secure against mob rule.

Time was when lynching appeared to be sectional, but now it is national—a blight upon our nation, mocking our laws and disgracing our Christianity. "With malice toward none but with charity for all" let us undertake the work of making the "law of the land" effective and supreme upon every foot of American soil—a shield to the innocent; and to the guilty, punishment swift and sure.

Shirley Chisholm
Presidential Campaign Speech
May 6, 1972

Ladies and gentlemen, I am very glad to be here this afternoon.

As all of you are well aware of the fact by now, inspite of what has been said about my candidacy; I indeed am a very serious candidate for the presidency of this country. It's recognized that it takes a little bit of time for people to get over a few psychological shocks now and then. But then, if we're going to be able to effect change within the system, even though said system has not given a lot of people hope because of color, sex or other factors, that they have to be people who are just merely Catholics and there have to be people who say, We dare. They have to be people who just say, look we're just as good as the rest of you and even though you may snicker and laugh, you're going to take a try at it.

So I'm out here, having lots of fun, giving a message to people in this country; a message that is sorely needed; a message which reflected itself last night in terms

of the unfortunate incident with respect to one of the other candidates who was running for this office - a clear indication of the malaise in America today, an indication that you certainly need new input on the top level in this country, that you certainly need the creative capacities and other kinds of solutions to peoples who have not had the opportunity to have some input in this government on the highest level.

So today I just want to talk a little bit about the whole economy. I want to say to you that we can't do anything about the problems confronting us here at home until we are able to end that atrocious war which takes 70 cents out of every dollar that we pay into the Federal Treasury. And thus, and thus part of the reason for the disquietude, the anxiety and the concerns of the American people have to do with the fact that their tax dollars that are being paid into the Federal Treasury are not being returned to them in terms of what it is that they should get out of this government, which is their government, and which is supposedly government of the people, by the people, and for the people.

The disastrous performance of the economy under the current administration can be largely understood as the result of the big business orientation of this government and its utter disregard for critical problems of the consumer. Millions of low-income Americans have deeply suffered from the administration's callous handling of the economy and the recession has, of course, created very tragic side effects: increased crime, increased welfare roles, and widespread despair among the poor and the unemployed of America over the moral intentions of this administration. And more and more Americans are beginning to realize how close the Nixon administration's alliance is with the huge corporate and business interest of this nation. They remember clearly when six days after his inauguration the president announced that the government would not intervene in price and wage discussions, and they remember very clearly when the administration calmly admitted that an increase in unemployment in America would be necessary to reduce inflation - and the result of this passivity towards the rich on one hand and the incomprehensible cold-bloodedness towards the worker and the poor on the other hand has been the worst possible economic crisis: virtually complete economic stagnation, increased and continuing inflation, record high unemployment, the first trade deficit since 1893, a huge balance of payment deficits, a world monetary crisis and the forced devaluation of the dollar. And the economic record of the administration is very clear and its statistics are appalling for the average American taxpayer.

The cost of living in America has risen under this administration at a rate double that during the previous one. Food prices have skyrocketed, the cost of owning a home has soared. Medical and hospital costs have now shot completely beyond control. Local transit fees have gone up 18 percent. Basic commodities such as copper and steel mill products increased in the first year of this administration to the percentage increase during the entire eight-year period from 1961 to 1968.

The policies of this administration have caused the largest increase in unemployment in over a decade, an increase from 3.5 percent to over 6 percent of the labor force, or two million jobless working right now in America. The unemployment rate for construction workers has more than doubled. The unemployment rate for manufacturing employees has almost doubled. The number of workers forced to live on unemployment compensation has doubled. The unemployment rate for black Americans has climbed to over 10 percent. Black teenage unemployment is at an intolerable 38 percent.

There is little sign that this administration has any real concern for the personal impact of unemployment in terms of relatives out of work, while prices have soared and the low-income worker has lost his job. The Nixon administration's bungling has virtually halted our nation's economic growth. The industrial production index fell steadily during the past three years and the real gross national product has declined. The cost of just borrowing has risen at an alarming rate, with interest rates soaring to the highest level in 100 years in this country. Housing construction has fallen more than 20 percent. State and local governments have been unable to borrow for vital public projects so they've had to close schools or to saddle the taxpayers with burdensome interest costs. This recession represents the fourth major recession in this country of the past 20 years - all having occurred under Republican administrations. But at the root of it all is the unique privileged relationship which these administrations have enjoyed with the nation's giant corporate and industrial interest, whose arrogant power has for too long been permitted to control Washington and thus all of our lives.

In the time-honored tradition of what is good for General Motors is good for the country, this administration refused to act when at the outset of its first year in office, big business coolly and confidently proceeded to announce huge price increases on a wide range of products. And as prices began to rise along the entire economic front, the administration then began to cut back on government spending in an effort to cool inflation. Which were the federal programs to be cut first of all? Federal assistance to libraries and related community services, education centers, aid for handicapped children, bilingual education, community health

centers, medical libraries and health research facilities, assistance to medical schools and consumer assistance. Everything that has to do with the conservation and preservation of the human resources in this country. Many jobs in these vital fields were abolished, people were thrown out of work. The Job Corps program was substantially reduced and the OEO office is just about gutted. And at the same time that this was going on, the administration energetically pushed those rates with enormously expensive programs benefiting the big business constituency. The ABM, the SST, the C5A, highway construction and the continued unjustifiable subsidies for corporate farms in this nation, while the Indians up on the reservations can't even get enough food to eat. And by slashing domestic programs, by continuing the 10 percent income tax surcharge and by its tight money policy of high interest rates, the Nixon Administration has by record - not by rhetoric, but by record - sacrificed the ambitions and energies of millions of low-income Americans: those who could at least afford to bear the burden of such a sacrifice.

We heard much in the 1968 campaign of the Nixon promises of jobs and training for black Americans, and of his firm support for black capitalism. One look at the record and at the ghettos of America's cities shows the utter emptiness of these campaign promises. The only action by the administration to promote black capitalism was the creation of an Office of Minority Business Enterprise in the Commerce Department, an office with no authority to make loans or to fund or supervise the programs. One after another the helpless officials of this program have not surprisingly been forced to quit the program. And with, the administration, having virtually destroyed any hope for improvement in the miserable economic position of poor of this country, Congress acted. It passed the law to provide hundreds of thousands of immediate jobs to the unemployed and the president vetoed it. Congress passed a bill providing daycare centers for children whose mothers could then join the workforce and get the kind of training and skills that are necessary to cope in a very highly automated society, because after all haven't many Americans been saying, "What are we going to do with the bums and the lazy people on welfare?" Well, we're here to tell you that they don't want welfare, and many of them have been on public assistance because of the presence in this country of an economy and of a system which relegated thousands of poor people to second-class citizenship status and people who never had the opportunity to really realize what this American dream everybody talks about is really meaningful to them. People don't want welfare, believe it or not, even poor people. They have pride, they have dignity, but if by virtue of a society that has had

inherent racism in the society, they have not had the same kind of equality of opportunities through the years; of course they're caught in a situation. We're in a highly automated society; they need training; they need skills and they don't have it because the unions won't even open up to let them in for apprentice and journeyman training programs. So we have to stop scape goating and generalizing about people and say that the republic is in trouble. It hasn't always treated everybody well. The administration then turned around, and showing where its real interest lay, acted to give billions of dollars of tax relief to business via the 10 percent investment credit, on top of its $4 billion a year depreciation reform. So this incredible story ends. If the chairman of the board of General Motors, earning a salary of three-quarters of a million of dollars in 1971, at the same time that the unemployed in Seattle have so little to eat that Japan feels obligated to ship some food over here to help them survive, gosh.

More and more thoughtful Americans, including a growing number of businessmen, have been shocked to learn of the economic inequality and exploitation, which is destroying the very fabric of American society. They have come to realize that this is a government of, by and for big business. The Nixon Cabinet and other top officials in the administration represent one of the greatest concentrations of individual wealth in the world. For the past one year I've been studying this and someday we'll be able to really see what I've come up with. And as such, they predictably resisted for so long, the use of the powers of the presidency in curbing the inflationary pressures that have been destroying the value of the American dollar. The economic philosophy of the administration is based on the principle that the business of America is business, and this being the case, the economic reality for the inexperienced and the untrained black man and the Indian and the Chicanos and the poor will have to continue to be: the last hired and the first fired.

This is an administration which ignores the social and psychological costs of its policies to the common man. It is an empty shell; the tool of slick advertising techniques; the prisoner of narrow political allegiances and the faithful servant of those privileged and selfish economic interests, which systematically block every attempt to narrow the gap between the rich and the poor in this country.
Rebuilding and revitalizing this society after four traumatic years depends more than anything else on meaningful changes in our economic priorities and this, the Nixon administration by its very nature can really never accept. A government so heavily dependent on a small clique of corporate millionaires, industrial polluters and privileged power brokers can never be seriously expected to concern itself with the day-to-day problems of the poor, the working man, the unemployed, black, the young or the elderly pensioner. I believe that

the future of our great society depends upon the ending of government by the conservative, repressive and selfish. It depends upon the ending of economic exploitation of the common man, both black and white, by those privileged powers which now rule in Washington.

Of course, for people who have not really known what it is to be poor or for people who do not really understand the significance of the rumblings of the veritable social revolution that is going through this country, it is impossible for you to understand the outrage - the outrage of people who are saying that they're sick and tired of tokenism. They're sick and tired of "see how far you've come." But they want their just share of that dream and that pride that everybody talks about. If you've traveled in this country you've seen how the Indians are living. Do you know that this country belongs to the Indians? And to see how these people are living and to realize that the latest Department of Labor statistics indicate quite clearly that close to 70 percent of these people do not live to see the age of 40. You could never come back here in this room and feel the same when you visit the reservations and see what is happening to these people. You go into the Appalachia region of the country, this most affluent society, and see the numbers, the numbers of poor Whites. And I have visited with them. They haven't seen politicians in 50 years, and many of them are a little bit surprised when they saw me because what am I doing, a black woman, coming into a poor white community? And I've said to them, "I'm concerned about your humanity. Of course, You're not going to see politicians; haven't you read the message? You're not important, you're poor. You'll see them every four years when it's time for votes." But to go into those areas and to see how those people are living in West Virginia and the hills of Kentucky: no floors, dirt. You walk into their place - it's dirt. No modern sanitary plumbing facilities, you have to go out in the back. America, this land of the free and the home of the brave. And to see how we can send so many care packages abroad. We have a sense, a deep sense of our moral obligation to people who are less fortunate than we are, and to thank God that we're able to extend a helping hand. But have you thought recently of sending care packages to America's children in the hinterlands of this country?

And so, I say that the time has come in America when those of us who by dint of economic security, financial stability, have a responsibility, a gut commitment if you will, to help in this country to readdress itself to the priorities of human beings first of all, particularly the human beings who are in need of so much help, particularly the helpless and the powerless. The time has come in America when we must recognize that vacuums in this society are being filled all over America by

white extremists and by black extremists and this should be a clear indication to all of us that you are not assuming your correct role of leadership because you're so contented, perhaps, in your own little worlds, that you don't even recognize that those who have been relatively helpless and/or powerless are taking over completely because they can't depend on you any longer to give a sense of direction and to take them by the hand and say, "Come along, we will help." The republic is in deep trouble. It takes a great many things for me to get upset, but I've never been so upset as I have been the past seven months as I've gone up and down the length and the breadth of this country, to realize that we just put $225 billion the other day into a space program. Where are we going? And in cities of this country to realize that so many thousands of Americans take two to three hours daily to go to work from their places of residence back home again. The whole day? That money should be utilized for the development of massive transportation facilities in this country in areas that at least have a population of 250,000 people or better. What are we building going up there for when right here on earth our people can't even get transportation to go to work. What madness are we on? And to watch how people have to get up at 4 o'clock in the morning in many areas of this country to get to work to a job that starts at 7 a.m. There's no reason for that.

Our priorities are all mixed up, ladies and gentlemen. This is why we need some people now with common sense. We need people who are not merely academicians and theoreticians and bureaucrats drawing up blueprints for change in this country, when these people have absolutely no attunement or sensitivity to the kinds of programs and projects that are necessary to help America. I'm not talking about black people. At least black people are just asking for in because they've been left out. But a lot of your own folks are saying what is wrong that government is not addressing itself to the needs of the American people, and I just hope that we really begin to realize what is really happening to all of us at this hour in America. The time has come when we can be no longer the passive recipients of whatever the politics or the morals of a nation may decree for us as a people. But if we have the courage of our convictions and if we believe in the Judeo-Christian doctrine, and if you believe just simply in man's humanity to man; if you believe that it is time to really save America's children, that a lot of us will go home and reassess our own commitments and our own priorities and move in a different sense of direction to help to save our country. The challenge is here for all of us. Will we merely continue just to use the powerless and the helpless as scapegoats, or using generalizations against them or about them? Or will we now take the bull by the horns and say that we have failed in certain areas but we will come together and

make the American dream, at least in this generation, become some kind of reality for lots of folks. Thank you.

THINK
ACTION

Power Anywhere Where There's People!

A Speech by Fred Hampton
(SPEECH DELIVERED AT OLIVET CHURCH, 1969)

Power anywhere where there's people. Power anywhere where there's people. Let me give you an example of teaching people. Basically, the way they learn is observation and participation. You know a lot of us go around and joke ourselves and believe that the masses have PhDs, but that's not true. And even if they did, it wouldn't make any difference. Because with some things, you have to learn by seeing it or either participating in it. And you know yourselves that there are people walking around your community today that have all types of degrees that should be at this meeting but are not here. Right? Because you can have as many degrees as a thermometer. If you don't have any practice, they you can't walk across the street and chew gum at the same time.

Let me tell you how Huey P. Newton, the leader, the organizer, the founder, the main man of the Black Panther Party, went about it.

The community had a problem out there in California. There was an intersection, a four-way intersection; a lot of people were getting killed, cars running over them, and so the people went down and redressed their grievances to the government. You've done it before. I know you people in the community have. And they came back and the pigs said "No! You can't have any." Oh, they don't usually say you can't have it. They've gotten a little hipper than that now. That's what those degrees on the thermometer will get you. They tell you "Okay, we'll deal with it. Why

don't you come back next meeting and waste some time?"And they get you wound up in an excursion of futility, and you be in a cycle of insaneness, and you be goin' back and goin' back, and goin' back, and goin' back so many times that you're already crazy.

So they tell you, they say, "Okay niggers, what you want?" And they you jump up and you say, "Well, it's been so long, we don't know what we want", and then you walk out of the meeting and you're gone and they say, "Well, you niggers had your chance, didn't you?"

Let me tell you what Huey P. Newton did.

Huey Newton went and got Bobby Seale, the chairman of the Black Panther Party on a national level. Bobby Seale got his 9mm, that's a pistol. Huey P. Newton got his shotgun and got some stop signs and got a hammer. Went down to the intersection, gave his shotgun to Bobby, and Bobby had his 9mm. He said, "You hold this shotgun. Anybody mess with us, blow their brains out." He put those stop signs up.

There were no more accidents, no more problems.

Now they had another situation. That's not that good, you see, because its two people dealing with a problem. Huey Newton and Bobby Seale, no matter how bad they may be, cannot deal with the problem. But let me explain to you who the real heroes are.

Next time, there was a similar situation, another four-way corner. Huey went and got Bobby, went and got his 9mm, got his shotgun, got his hammer and got more stop signs. Placed those stop signs up, gave the shotgun to Bobby, told Bobby "If anybody mess with us while were putting these stop signs up, protect the people and blow their brains out." What did the people do? They observed it again. They participated in it. Next time they had another four-way intersection. Problems there; they had accidents and death. This time, the people in the community went and got their shotguns, got their hammers, got their stop signs.

Now, let me show you how were gonna try to do it in the Black Panther Party here. We just got back from the south side. We went out there. We went out there and we got to arguing with the pigs or the pigs got to arguing-he said, "Well, Chairman Fred, you supposed to be so bad, why don't you go and shoot some of those policemen? You always talking about you got your guns and got this, why don't you go shoot some of them?"

And I've said, "You've just broken a rule. As a matter of fact, even though you have on a uniform it doesn't make me any difference. Because I don't care if you got on nine uniforms, and 100 badges. When you step outside the realm of legality and into the realm of illegality, then I feel that you should be arrested." And I told him, "You being what they call the law of entrapment, you tried to make me do something that was wrong, you encouraged me, you tried to incite me to shoot a pig. And that ain't cool, Brother, you know the law, don't you?"

I told that pig that, I told him "You got a gun, pig?" I told him, "You gotta get your hands up

against the wall. We're gonna do what they call a citizen's arrest." This fool don't know what this is. I said, "Now you be just as calm as you can and don't make too many quick moves, cause we don't wanna have to hit you."

And I told him like he always told us, I told him, "Well, I'm here to protect you. Don't worry about a thing, 'm here for your benefit." So I sent another Brother to call the pigs. You gotta do that in a citizen's arrest. He called the pigs. Here come the pigs with carbines and shotguns, walkin' out there. They came out there talking about how they're gonna arrest Chairman Fred. And I said, "No fool. This is the man you got to arrest. He's the one that broke the law." And what did they do? They bugged their eyes, and they couldn't stand it. You know what they did? They were so mad, they were so angry that they told me to leave.

And what happened? All those people were out there on 63rd Street. What did they do? They were around there laughing and talking with me while I was making the arrest. They looked at me while I was rapping and heard me while I was rapping. So the next time that the pig comes on 63rd Street, because of the thing that our Minister of Defense calls observation and participation, that pig might be arrested by anybody!

So what did we do? We were out there educating the people. How did we educate them? Basically, the way people learn, by observation and participation. And that's what we're trying to do. That's what we got to do here in this community. And a lot of people don't understand, but there are three basic things that you got to do anytime you intend to have yourself a successful revolution.

A lot of people get the word revolution mixed up and they think revolutions a bad word. Revolution is nothing but like having a sore on your body and then you put something on that sore to cure that infection. And Im telling you that were living in an infectious society right now. I'm telling you that were living in a sick society. And anybody that endorses integrating into this sick society before it's cleaned up is a man who's committing a crime against the people.

If you walk past a hospital room and see a sign that says "Contaminated" and then you try to lead people into that room, either those people are mighty dumb, you understand me, cause if they weren't, they'd tell you that you are an unfair, unjust leader that does not have your followers' interests in mind. And what we're saying is simply that leaders have got to become, we've got to start making them accountable for what they do. They're goin' around talking about so-and-so's an Uncle Tom so we're gonna open up a cultural center and teach him what blackness is. And this n****r is more aware than you and me and Malcolm and Martin Luther King and everybody else put together. That's right. They're the ones that are most aware. They're most aware, cause they're the ones that are gonna open up the center. They're gonna tell you where bones come from in Africa that you can't even pronounce the names. That's right. They'll be telling you about Chaka, the leader of the Bantu freedom fighters, and Jomo Kenyatta, those dingo-dingas. They'll be running all of that down to you. They know about it all. But the point is they do what they're doing because it is beneficial and it is profitable for them.

You see, people get involved in a lot of things that's profitable to them, and we've got to make it less profitable. We've got to make it less beneficial. I'm saying that any program that's brought

into our community should be analyzed by the people of that community. It should be analyzed to see that it meets the relevant needs of that community. We don't need no n*****s coming into our community to be having no company to open business for the n*****s. There's too many n*****s in our community that can't get crackers out of the business that they're gonna open.

We got to face some facts. That the masses are poor, that the masses belong to what you call the lower class, and when I talk about the masses, I'm talking about the white masses, I'm talking about the black masses, and the brown masses, and the yellow masses, too. We've got to face the fact that some people say you fight fire best with fire, but we say you put fire out best with water. We say you don't fight racism with racism. We're gonna fight racism with solidarity. We say you don't fight capitalism with no black capitalism; you fight capitalism with socialism.

We ain't gonna fight no reactionary pigs who run up and down the street being reactionary; we're gonna organize and dedicate ourselves to revolutionary political power and teach ourselves the specific needs of resisting the power structure, arm ourselves, and we're gonna fight reactionary pigs with INTERNATIONAL PROLETARIAN REVOLUTION. That's what it has to be. The people have to have the power: it belongs to the people.

We have to understand very clearly that there's a man in our community called a capitalist. Sometimes he's black and sometimes he's white. But that man has to be driven out of our community, because anybody who comes into the community to make profit off the people by exploiting them can be defined as a capitalist. And we don't care how many programs they have, how long a dashiki they have. Because political power does not flow from the sleeve of a dashiki; political power flows from the barrel of a gun. It flows from the barrel of a gun!

A lot of us running around talking about politics don't even know what politics is. Did you ever see something and pull it and you take it as far as you can and it almost outstretches itself and it goes into something else? If you take it so far that it is two things? As a matter of fact, some things if you stretch it so far, it'll be another thing. Did you ever cook something so long that it turns into something else? Ain't that right?

That's what we're talking about with politics.

That politics ain't nothing, but if you stretch it so long that it can't go no further, then you know what you got on your hands? You got an antagonistic contradiction. And when you take that contradiction to the highest level and stretch it as far as you can stretch it, you got what you call war. Politics is war without bloodshed, and war is politics with bloodshed. If you don't understand that, you can be a Democrat, Republican, you can be Independent, you can be anything you want to, you ain't nothing.

We don't want any of those n*****s and any of these hunkies and nobody else, radicals or nobody talking about, "I'm on the Independence ticket." That means you sell out the republicans; Independent means you're out for graft and you'll sell out to the highest bidder. You understand?

We want people who want to run on the People's Party, because the people are gonna run it whether they like it or not. The people have proved that they can run it. They run it in China,

they're gonna run it right here. They can call it what they want to, they can talk about it. They can call it communism, and think that that's gonna scare somebody, but it ain't gonna scare nobody.

We had the same thing happen out on 37th Road. They came out to 37th road where our Breakfast for children program is, and started getting those women who were kind of older, around 58---that's, you know, I call that older cause Im young. I aint 20, right, right! But you see, they're gonna get them and brainwash them. And you ain't seen nothin till you see one of them beautiful Sisters with their hair kinda startin getting grey, and they ain't got many teeth, and they were tearin' them policemen up! They were tearing em up! The pigs would come up to them and say "You like communism?"

The pigs would come up to them and say, "You scared of communism?" And the Sisters would say, "No scared of it, I ain't never heard of it."

"You like socialism?"

"No scared of it. I ain't never heard of it."

The pigs, they be crackin' up, because they enjoyed seeing these people frightened of these words.

"You like capitalism?"

Yeah, well, that's what I live with. I like it.

"You like the Breakfast For Children program, n****r?" "Yeah, I like it."
And the pigs say, "Oh-oh." The pigs say, "Well, the Breakfast For Children program is a socialistic program. It's a communistic program."

And the women said, "Well, I tell you what, boy. I've been knowing you since you were knee- high to a grasshopper, n****r. And I don't know if I like communism and I don't know if I like socialism. But I know that that Breakfast For Children program feeds my kids, n****r. And if you put your hands on that Breakfast For Children program, I'm gonna come off this can and I'm gonna beat your ass like a ...."

That's what they be saying. That's what they be saying, and it is a beautiful thing. And that's what the Breakfast For Children program is. A lot of people think it is charity, but what does it do? It takes the people from a stage to another stage. Any program that's revolution- ary is an advancing program. Revolution is change. Honey, if you just keep on changing, before you know it, in fact, not even knowing what socialism is, you don't have to know what it is, they're endorsing it, they're participating in it, and they're supporting socialism.

And a lot of people will tell you, way, well, the people don't have any theory, they need some theory. They need some theory even if they don't have any practice. And the Black Panther Party tells you that if a man tells you that he's the type of man who has you buying candy bars and eating the wrapping and throwing the candy away, he'd have you walking east when you're supposed to be walking West. It's true. If you listen to what the pig says, you be walkin' outside when the sun is shining with your umbrella over your head. And when it's raining you'll be goin' outside leaving your umbrella inside. That's right. You gotta get it together. I'm saying that's what they have you doing.

Now, what do WE do? We say that the Breakfast For Children pro- gram is a socialistic program. It teaches the people basically that by practice, we thought up and let them practice that theory and inspect that theory. What's more important? You learn something just like everybody else.

Let me try to break it down to you.

You say this Brother here goes to school 8 years to be an auto me- chanic. And that teacher who used to be an auto mechanic, he tells him, "Well, n****r, you gotta go on what we call on-the- job-train- ing." And he says, "Damn, with all this theory I got, I gotta go to on- the-job-training? What for?"

He said, "On on-the-job-training he works with me. Ive been here for 20 years. When I started work, they didn't even have auto mechanics. I ain't got no theory, I just got a whole bunch of practice."

What happened? A car came in making a whole lot of funny noise. This Brother here go get his book. He on page one, he ain't got to page 200. I'm sitting here listening to the car. He says, "What do you think it is?"

I say, "I think it's the carburetor."

He says, "No I don't see anywhere in here where it says a carburetor make no noise like that." And he says, "How do you know it's the carburetor?"

I said, "Well, n****r, with all them degrees as many as a thermometer, around 20 years ago, 19 to be exact, I was listening to the same kind of noise. And what I did was I took apart the voltage regulator and it wasn't that. Then I took apart the alternator and it wasn't that. I took apart the generator brushes and it wasn't that. I took apart the generator and it wasn't that. I took apart the generator and it wasn't even that. After I took apart all that I finally got to the carburetor and when I got to the carburetor I found that that's what it was. And I told myself that 'fool, next time you hear this sound you better take apart the carburetor first.'"

How did he learn? He learned through practice.

I don't care how much theory you got, if it don't have any practice applied to it, then that theory happens to be irrelevant. Right? Any theory you get, practice it. And when you practice it you make some mistakes. When you make a mistake, you correct that theory, and then it will be

corrected theory that will be able to be applied and used in any situation. That's what we've got to be able to do.

Every time I speak in a church I always try to say something, you know, about Martin Luther King. I have a lot of respect for Martin Luther King. I think he was one of the greatest orators that the country ever produced. And I listened to anyone who speaks well, because I like to listen to that. Martin Luther King said that it might look dark sometime, and it might look dark over here on the North Side. Maybe you thought the room was going to be packed with people and maybe you thought you might have to turn some people away and you might not have enough people here. Maybe some of the people you think should be here are not here and you think that, well if they're not here then it won't be as good as we thought it could have been. And maybe you thought that you need more people here than you have here. Maybe you think that the pigs are going to be able to pressure you and put enough pressure to squash your movement even before it starts. But Martin Luther King said that he heard somewhere that only when it is dark enough can you see the stars. And we're not worried about it being dark. He said that the arm of the moral universe is long, but it bends toward heaven.

We got Huey P. Newton in jail, and Eldridge Cleaver underground. And Alprentice Bunchy Carter has been murdered; Bobby Hutton and John Huggins been murdered. And a lot of people think that the Black Panther Party in a sense is giving up. But let us say this: That we've made the kind of commitment to the people that hardly anyone else has ever made.

We have decided that although some of us come from what some of you would call petty- bourgeois families, though some of us could be in a sense on what you call the mountaintop. We could be integrated into the society working with people that we may never have a chance to work with. Maybe we could be on the mountaintop and maybe we wouldn't have to be hidin' when we go to speak places like this. Maybe we wouldn't have to worry about court cases and going to jail and being sick. We say that even though all of those luxuries exist on the mountaintop, we understand that you people and your problems are right here in the valley.

We in the Black Panther Party, because of our dedication and understanding, went into the valley knowing that the people are in the valley, knowing that our plight is the same plight as the people in the valley, knowing that our enemies are on the mountain, to our friends are in the valley, and even though its nice to be on the mountaintop, we're going back to the valley. Because we understand that there's work to be done in the valley, and when we get through with this work in the valley, then we got to go to the mountaintop. We're going to the mountaintop because there's a motherfucker on the mountaintop that's playing King, and he's been bullshitting us. And we've got to go up on the mountain top not for the purpose of living his life style and living like he lives. We've got to go up on the mountain top to make this motherfucker understand, goddamnit, that we are coming from the valley!

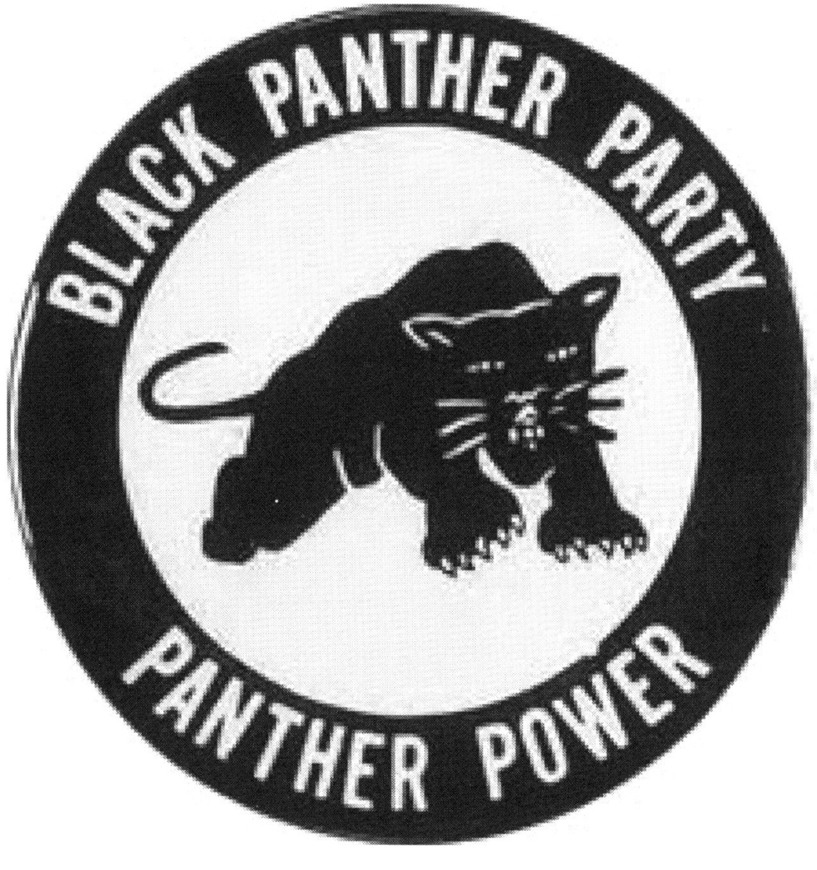
BLACK PANTHER PARTY
PANTHER POWER

W.E.B. DU BOIS

"A Negro Nation Within a Nation"
Du Bois gave this speech on June 26, 1934 as he re-
signed from the NAACP.

No MORE CRITICAL SITUATION ever faced the Negroes of America than that of today-not in 1830, nor in 1861, nor in 1867. More than ever the appeal of the Negro for elementary justice falls on deaf ears.

Three-fourths of us are disfranchised; yet no writer on democratic reform, no third-party movement says a word about Negroes. The Bull Moose crusade in 1912 refused to notice them; the La Follette uprising in 1924 was hardly aware of them; the Socialists still keep them in the background. Negro children are systematically denied education; when the National Educational Association asks for federal aid to education it permits discrimination to be perpetuated by the present local authorities. Once or twice a month Negroes convicted of no crime are openly and publicly lynched, and even burned; yet a National Crime Convention is brought to perfunctory and unwilling notice of this only by mass picketing and all but illegal agitation. When a man with every qualification is refused a position simply because his great-grandfather was black, there is not a ripple of comment or protest.

Long before the depression Negroes in the South were losing "Negro" jobs, those assigned them by common custom-poorly paid and largely undesirable toil, but nevertheless life-supporting. New techniques, new enterprises, mass production, impersonal ownership and control have been largely displacing the skilled white and Negro worker in tobacco manufacturing, in iron and steel, in lumbering and mining, and in transportation. Negroes are now restricted more and more to common labor and domestic service of the lowest paid and worst kind. In textile, chemical and other manufactures Negroes were from the first nearly excluded, and just as slavery kept the poor white out of profitable agriculture, so freedom prevents the poor Negro from finding a place in manufacturing. The worldwide decline in agriculture has moreover carried the mass of black farmers, despite heroic endeavor among the few, down to the level of landless tenants and peons.

The World War and its wild aftermath seemed for a moment to open a new door; two million black workers rushed North to work in iron and steel, make automobiles and pack meat, build houses and do the heavy toil in factories. They met first the closed trade union which excluded them from the best paid jobs and pushed them into the low-wage gutter, denied them homes and mobbed them. Then they met the depression.

Since 1929 Negro workers, like white workers, have lost their jobs, have had mortgages foreclosed on their farms and homes, have used up their small savings. But, in the case of the Negro worker, everything has been worse in larger or smaller degree; the loss has been greater and more permanent. Technological displacement, which began before the depression, has been accelerated, while unemployment and falling wages struck black men sooner, went to lower levels and will last longer.

The colored people of America are coming to face the fact quite calmly that most white Americans do not like them, and are planning neither for their survival, nor for their definite future if it involves free, self-assertive modern manhood. This does not mean all Americans. A saving few are worried about the Negro problem; a still larger group are not ill-disposed, but they fear prevailing public opinion. The great mass of Americans are, however, merely representatives of average humanity. They muddle along with their own affairs and scarcely can be expected to take seriously the affairs of strangers or people whom they partly fear and partly despise.

For many years it was the theory of most Negro leaders that this attitude was the insensibility of ignorance and inexperience, that white America did not know of or realize the continuing plight of the Negro. Accordingly, for the latter two decades, we have striven by book and periodical, by speech and appeal, by various dramatic methods of agitation, to put the essential facts before the American people. Today there can be no doubt that Americans know the facts; and yet they remain for the most part indifferent and unmoved.

The peculiar position of Negroes in America offers an opportunity. Negroes today cast probably 2,000,000 votes in a total of 40,000,000 and their vote will increase. This gives them, particularly in northern cities, and at critical times, a chance to hold a very considerable balance of power and the mere threat of this being used intelligently and with determination may often mean much. The consuming power of 2,800,000 Negro families has recently been estimated at $166,000,000 a month—a tremendous power when intelligently directed. Their manpower as laborers probably equals that of Mexico or Yugoslavia. Their illiteracy is much lower than that of Spain or Italy. Their estimated per capita wealth about equals that of Japan.

For a nation with this start in culture and efficiency to sit down and await the salvation of a white God is idiotic. With the use of their political power, their power as consumers, and their brainpower, added to that chance of personal appeal which proximity and neighborhood always give to human to human beings, Negroes can develop in the United States an economic nation within a nation, able to work through inner cooperation to found its own institutions, to educate its genius, and at the same time, without mob violence or extremes of race hatred, to keep in helpful touch and cooperate with the mass of the nation. This has happened more often than most people realize, in the case of groups not so obviously separated from the mass of people as are American Negroes. It must happen in our case or there is no hope for the Negro in America.

Any movement toward such a program is today hindered by the absurd Negro philosophy of Scatter, Suppress, Wait, Escape. There are even many of our educated young leaders who think that because the Negro problem is not in evidence where there are few or no Negroes, this indicates a way out! They think that the problem of race can be settled by ignoring it and suppressing all reference to it. They think that we have only to 3wait in silence for the white people to settle the problem for us; and finally and predominantly, they think that the problem of twelve million Negro people, mostly poor, ignorant workers, is going to be settled by having their more educated and wealthy classes gradually and continually escape from their race into the mass of the American people, leaving the rest to sink, suffer and die.

Proponents of this program claim, with much reason, that the plight of the masses is not the fault of the emerging classes. For the slavery and exploitation that reduced Negroes to their present level or at any rate hindered them from rising, the white world is to blame. Since the age-long process of raising a group is through the escape of its upper class into welcome fellowship with risen peoples, the Negro intelligentsia would submerge itself if it bent its back to the task of lifting the mass of people. There is logic in this answer, but futile logic.

If the leading Negro classes cannot assume and bear the uplift of their own proletariat, they are doomed for all time. It is not a case of ethics; it is a plain case of necessity. The method by which this may be done is, first, for the American Negro to achieve a new economic solidarity.

It may be said that this matter of a nation within a nation has already been partially accomplished in the organization of the Negro church, the Negro school and the Negro retail business, and despite all the justly due criticism, the result has been astonishing. The great majority of American Negroes are divided not only for religious but for a large number of social purposes into self-supporting economic units, self-governed, self-directed. The greatest difficulty is that these organizations have no logical and reasonable standards and do not attract the fines, most vigorous and best educated Negroes. When all these things are taken into consideration it becomes clearer to more and more American Negroes that, through voluntary and increased segregation, by careful autonomy and planned economic organization, they may build so strong and efficient a unit that twelve million men can no longer be refused fellowship and equality in the United States.

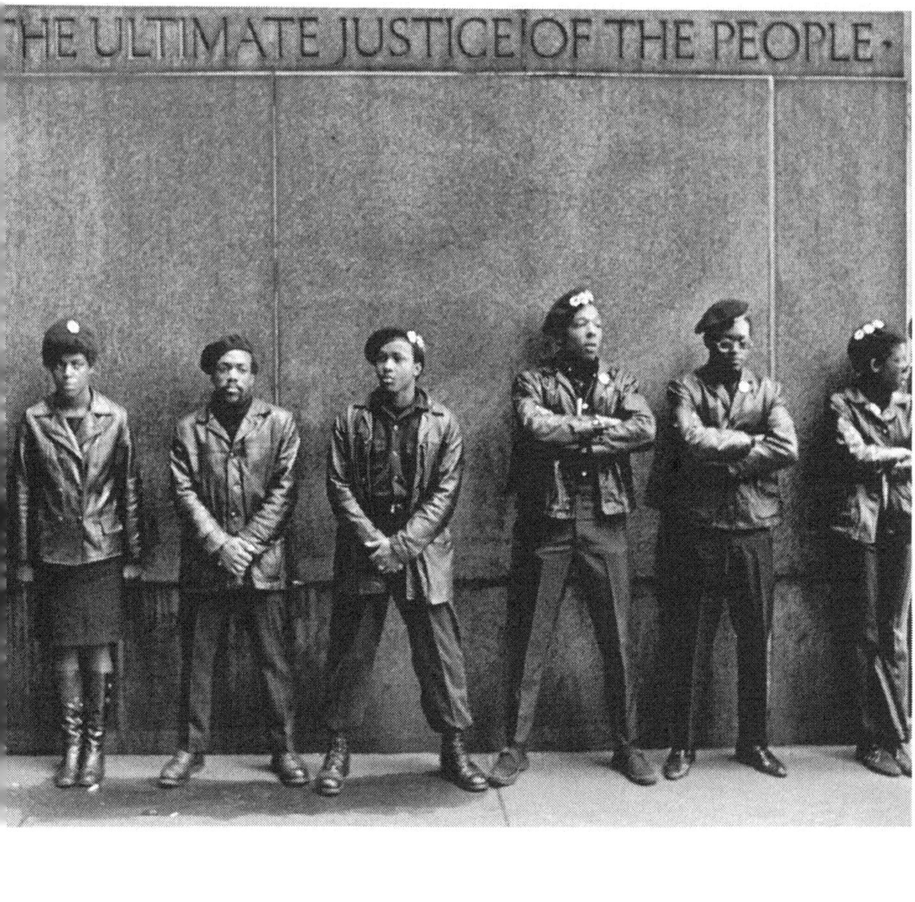
THE ULTIMATE JUSTICE OF THE PEOPLE

Booker T. Washington
Delivers the 1895 Atlanta Compromise Speech

On September 18, 1895, African-American spokesman and leader Booker T. Washington spoke before a predominantly white audience at the Cotton States and International Exposition in Atlanta. His "Atlanta Compromise" address, as it came to be called, was one of the most important and influential speeches in American history. Although the organizers of the exposition worried that "public sentiment was not prepared for such an advanced step," they decided that inviting a black speaker would impress Northern visitors with the evidence of racial progress in the South. Washington soothed his listeners' concerns about "uppity" blacks by claiming that his race would content itself with living "by the productions of our hands."

Mr. President and Gentlemen of the Board of Directors and Citizens:
One-third of the population of the South is of the Negro race. No enterprise seeking the material, civil, or moral welfare of this section can disregard this element of our population and reach the highest success. I but convey to you, Mr. President and Directors, the sentiment of the masses of my race when I say that in no way have the value and manhood of the American Negro been more fittingly and generously recognized than by the managers of this magnificent Exposition at every stage of its progress. It is a recognition that will do more to cement the friendship of the two races than any occurrence since the dawn of our freedom.

Not only this, but the opportunity here afforded will awaken among us a new era of industrial progress. Ignorant and inexperienced, it is not strange that in the first years of our new life we began at the top instead of at the bottom; that a seat in Congress or the state legislature was more sought than real estate or industrial skill; that the political convention or stump speaking had more attractions than starting a dairy farm or truck garden. A ship lost at sea for many days suddenly sighted a friendly vessel. From the mast of the unfortunate vessel was seen a signal, "Water, water; we die of thirst!" The answer from the friendly vessel at once came back, "Cast down your bucket where you are." A second time the signal, "Water, water; send us water!" ran up from the distressed vessel, and was answered, "Cast down your bucket where you are." And a third and fourth signal for water was answered, "Cast down your bucket where you are." The captain of the distressed vessel, at last heeding the injunction, cast down his bucket, and it came up full of fresh, sparkling water from the mouth of the Amazon River. To those of my race who depend on bettering their condition in a foreign land or who underestimate the importance of cultivating friendly relations with the Southern white man, who is their next-door neighbor, I would say: "Cast down your bucket where you are"— cast it down in making friends in every manly way of the people of all races by whom we are surrounded.

Cast it down in agriculture, mechanics, in commerce, in domestic service, and in the professions. And in this connection it is well to bear in mind that whatever other sins the South may be called to bear, when it comes to business, pure and simple, it is in the South that the Negro is given a man's chance in the commercial world, and in nothing is this Exposition more eloquent than in emphasizing this chance. Our greatest danger is that in the great leap from slavery to freedom we may overlook the fact that the masses of us are to live by the productions of our hands, and fail to keep in mind that we shall prosper in proportion as we learn to dignify and glorify common labour, and put brains and skill into the common occupations of life; shall prosper in proportion as we learn to draw the line between the superficial and the substantial, the ornamental gewgaws of life and the useful. No race can prosper till it learns that there is as much dignity in tilling a field as in writing a poem. It is at the bottom of life we must begin, and not at the top. Nor should we permit our grievances to overshadow our opportunities.

To those of the white race who look to the incoming of those of foreign birth and strange tongue and habits for the prosperity of the South, were I permitted I would repeat what I say to my own race, "Cast down your bucket where you are." Cast it down among the eight millions of Negroes whose habits you know, whose fidelity and love you have tested in days when to have proved treacherous meant the ruin of your firesides. Cast down your bucket among these people who have, without strikes and labour wars, tilled your fields, cleared your forests, builded your railroads and cities, and brought forth treasures from the bowels of the earth, and helped make possible this magnificent representation of the progress of the South. Casting down your bucket among my people, helping and encouraging them as you are doing on these grounds, and to education of head, hand, and heart, you will find that they will buy your surplus land, make blossom the waste places in your fields, and run your factories. While doing this, you can be sure in the future, as in the past, that you and your families will be surrounded by the most patient, faithful, law-abiding, and unresentful people that the world has seen. As we have proved our loyalty to you in the past, in nursing your children, watching by the sick-bed of your mothers and fathers, and often following them with tear-dimmed eyes to their graves, so in the future, in our humble way, we shall stand by you with a devotion that no foreigner can approach, ready to lay down our lives, if need be, in defense of yours, interlacing our industrial, commercial, civil, and religious life with yours in a way that shall make the interests of both races one. In all things that are purely social we can be as separate as the fingers, yet one as the hand in all things essential to mutual progress.

There is no defense or security for any of us except in the highest intelligence and development of all. If anywhere there are efforts tending to curtail the fullest growth of the Negro, let these efforts be turned into stimulating, encouraging, and making him the most useful and intelligent citizen. Effort or means so invested will pay a thousand per cent interest. These efforts will be twice blessed—blessing him that gives and him that takes.

There is no escape through law of man or God from the inevitable:

The laws of changeless justice bind Oppressor with oppressed;

And close as sin and suffering joined We march to fate abreast...

Nearly sixteen millions of hands will aid you in pulling the load upward, or they will pull against you the load downward. We shall constitute one-third and more of the ignorance and crime of the South, or one-third [of] its intelligence and progress; we shall contribute one-third to the business and industrial prosperity of the South, or we shall prove a veritable body of death, stagnating, depressing, retarding every effort to advance the body politic.

Gentlemen of the Exposition, as we present to you our humble effort at an exhibition of our progress, you must not expect overmuch. Starting thirty years ago with ownership here and there in a few quilts and pumpkins and chickens (gathered from miscellaneous sources), remember the path that has led from these to the inventions and production of agricultural implements, buggies, steam-engines, newspapers, books, statuary, carving, paintings, the management of drug stores and banks, has not been trodden without contact with thorns and thistles. While we take pride in what we exhibit as a result of our independent efforts, we do not for a moment forget that our part in this exhibition would fall far short of your expectations but for the constant help that has come to our educational life, not only from the Southern states, but especially from Northern philanthropists, who have made their gifts a constant stream of blessing and encouragement.

The wisest among my race understand that the agitation of questions of social equality is the extremest folly, and that progress in the enjoyment of all the privileges that will come to us must be the result of severe and constant struggle rather than of artificial forcing. No race that has anything to contribute to the markets of the world is long in any degree ostracized. It is important and right that all privileges of the law be ours, but it is vastly more important that we be prepared for the exercise of these privileges.

The opportunity to earn a dollar in a factory just now is worth infinitely more than the opportunity to spend a dollar in an opera-house.

In conclusion, may I repeat that nothing in thirty years has given us more hope and encouragement, and drawn us so near to you of the white race, as this opportunity offered by the Exposition; and here bending, as it were, over the altar that represents the results of the struggles of your race and mine, both starting practically empty-handed three decades ago, I pledge that in your effort to work out the great and intricate problem which God has laid at the doors of the South, you shall have at all times the patient, sympathetic help of my race; only let this be constantly in mind, that, while from representations in these buildings of the product of field, of forest, of mine, of factory, letters, and art, much good will come, yet far above and beyond material benefits will be that higher good, that, let us pray God, will come, in a blotting out of sectional differences and racial animosities and suspicions, in a determination to administer absolute justice, in a willing obedience among all classes to the mandates of law. This, coupled with our material prosperity, will bring into our beloved South a new heaven and a new earth.

THINK

CRITICALLY

Marcus Garvey
Negro Political Union

October 26, 1924, We are assembled here this afternoon under the auspices of the Universal Negro Political Union? This is the first of a series of meetings that the Union will stage in Liberty Hall during the present political campaign for the purpose of educating the members of the Union, the members of the Universal Negro Improvement Association and the Negroes of Harlem generally as to the real meaning of politics and at the same time to prepare them to vote during the forthcoming national election.

Politics is an important science. It is that science that protects those human rights that are not protected by law. It is the only medium or weapon need, and for that reason the delegates representing the Negro peoples, not l this country, but all over the world thought it wise, good and proper this time we should organize within the Universal Negro Improvement Association, as an auxiliary, a distinct political institution that would be charged with the duty of protecting and looking after the political rights of the people there everywhere. The Union is firmly established all over this country. We have branches at the present time, organized by the 1,400 branches of the Universal Negro Improvement Association, all over the country, and we have given out from executive headquarters a program that is going to be followed during this campaign for the national election, and we want the Negroes of Harlem to be well acquainted with what has been done and what should be done. It is for that reason that we call you here this afternoon.

TO BE TRICKED NO LONGER

The time has come for the Negro to stop allowing himself to be bamboozled and tricked and fooled by Tom, Dick and Harry. The time has come for him to settle down on a policy of his own, in politics, in religion, in education, in society, in every walk of life. The Jew has a policy in politics and religion. Every group has a policy in politics and religion, and we think the time has come for the Negro to have a policy in politics and religion. We have laid down already our religious policy. That was widely discussed during the convention and widely promulgated as a doctrine all over the world; and now we are laying down our political policy, and we want you to follow us lily and attentively this afternoon as we enunciate this policy in good old Liberty Hall.

I feel sure that those of you who are members of the Universal Negro Improvement Association and those of you who are members of the Universal

Negro Political Union are going to exercise the franchise with telling effect during this election period. We want to say at the outset, however, that the Universal Negro Political Union is different from all other Negro political organizations. Nobody gives us any money. We support our own policies and pay for them, so that we can be in a position to talk and to demand what we want. (Applause.) Nobody pays us to talk. They could not pay us to talk. We talk because we feel the righteousness of our expressions. We talk because we feel it our responsibility to talk in the interests of the people m we represent.

NO MONEY TAKES

You know some fellows thought we would never get into politics, but we take time doing everything. As we took time before we bought a ship, so we take time before we enter politics. But there is one thing about the Universal Negro Improvement Association and all things identified with the Universal Negro Improvement Association--when we enter a thing we are in it to the death. (Applause.) And we are going to see it through. And so you realize that all over this country at this time the Universal Negro Political Union is taking a stand.... The first speaker of the afternoon is Sir William Sherrill. Sir William Sherrill is the chairman of the American wing of the Universal Negro Political Union. You know the Universal Negro Political Union is as universal as the Universal Negro Political [Improvement?] Association. I am the Universal chairman and Mr. Sherrill is the chairman of the American wing of the Union. The Universal Negro Political Union has as much interest in the politics of Haiti and Barbados and Trinidad and British Guiana and Jamaica as in any African state. Our duty is to put in office men who we believe will serve the interests of the Negro race. So when the next election comes off in Trinidad you are going to find candidates representing the Universal Negro Political Union just as we have candidates here indorsed by the Universal Negro Political Union. When the next political campaign starts in Jamaica we are going to see to it that fourteen black men get into the legislative council of Jamaica backed by the Universal Negro Political Union. (Applause.) And so Barbados and British Guiana. We are just out in politics now and we are going to clean up everything for justice and righteousness. (Applause.)

THINK BLACK

ITS OKAY...

Made in the USA
Columbia, SC
07 December 2024